W9-CEY-903

FUDDY MEERS

BY
DAVID LINDSAY-ABAIRE

★

★

DRAMATISTS
PLAY SERVICE
INC.

FUDDY MEERS was produced by Manhattan Theatre Club (Lynne Meadow, Artistic Director; Barry Grove, Executive Producer) in New York City on October 12, 1999. It was directed by David Petrarca; the set and costume design were by Santo Loquasto; the lighting design was by Brian MacDevitt; the sound design was by Bruce Ellman; the original music was by Jason Robert Brown; the fight direction was by Rick Sordelet; and the production stage manager was Thea Bradshaw Gillies. The cast was as follows:

CLAIRE	J. Smith-Cameron
RICHARD	Robert Stanton
KENNY	Keith Nobbs
LIMPING MAN	Patrick Breen
GERTIE	Marylouise Burke
MILLET	Mark McKinney
HEIDI	Lisa Gorlitsky

FUDDY MEERS subsequently transferred to the Minetta Lane Theatre in New York City, produced by the Manhattan Theatre Club and Jean Doumanian Productions, on January 27, 2000. It was directed by David Petrarca; the set and costume design were by Santo Loquasto; the lighting design was by Brian MacDevitt; the sound design was by Bruce Ellman; the original music was by Jason Robert Brown; the fight direction was by Rick Sordelet; and the production stage manager was Thea Bradshaw Gillies. The cast was as follows:

CLAIRE	J. Smith-Cameron
RICHARD	Robert Stanton
KENNY	Keith Nobbs
LIMPING MAN	Patrick Breen
GERTIE	Marylouise Burke
MILLET	John Christopher Jones
HEIDI	Clea Lewis

CHARACTERS

CLAIRE — about 40, a generally sunny woman with amnesia.

RICHARD — about 40, a chatty, friendly, sometimes nervous man.

KENNY — 17, a troubled teen.

LIMPING MAN — about 40, a lisping, limping, half-blind, half-deaf man with secrets.

GERTIE — 60's, a clear-headed lady who's had a stroke and can't speak properly.

MILLET — 30's or 40's, an odd man with a puppet.

HEIDI — 30's or 40's, a tough woman in uniform.

FUDDY MEERS

ACT ONE

SCENE 1

Alarm clock ringing. Lights up on Claire in a bed. She tries to open her eyes. She looks at the ringing clock, confused. She takes in the room as if for the first time.

Richard, in a robe, enters with a mug of coffee, which he puts on Claire's side table.

RICHARD.   Good morning, huckleberry! How'd you sleep? You sleep well?!
CLAIRE.   I'm not sure.
RICHARD.   *(Shuts alarm off.)* I think you did. You snored a lot. You slept soundly.
CLAIRE.   That's good.
RICHARD.   Sounded soundly. Maybe you had bad dreams though. *(He draws the curtains. Sun pours into the room. Claire squints at the sunlight.)*
CLAIRE.   I don't remember dreaming.
RICHARD.   *(Opens closet and flips through clothes.)* No, of course not. But you did. We all do. I dreamt I was a soccer ball and everyone kept kicking me. Whaddaya suppose that meant?
CLAIRE.   I don't know.
RICHARD.   Oh well. *(Holds up dress.)* How about this today?
CLAIRE.   You mean for me?
RICHARD.   You like this dress.

CLAIRE. Oh, it's hideous.

RICHARD. You wear it all the time. You wore it to Jackie's Thanksgiving. *(Motions to coffee.)* That's your coffee. You can drink it.

CLAIRE. Who's Jackie?

RICHARD. Your cousin.

CLAIRE. Oh. *(Takes coffee.)* Aren't you having coffee?

RICHARD. I don't drink coffee. I had some juice.

CLAIRE. Oh, juice is nice.

RICHARD. No, you don't like juice, sweetheart.

CLAIRE. I don't?

RICHARD. No.

CLAIRE. I don't think I like that dress.

RICHARD. You do.

CLAIRE. I don't.

RICHARD. You do, darling. You like it very much.

CLAIRE. This is very unsettling. *(Kenny ducks in. He's seventeen.)*

KENNY. I don't need a ride. I'm taking the bus.

RICHARD. Did you feed the dog?

KENNY. No.

RICHARD. Don't forget, Kenny. Yesterday you forgot.

KENNY. *(As he exits.)* That dog's a fat hunk of shit.

RICHARD. That's Kenny.

CLAIRE. He smells like ribbon candy.

RICHARD. He smokes marijuana.

CLAIRE. That can't be good for him.

RICHARD. I'm hoping it's a phase. *(Picking up puzzle books.)* I'm throwing out these search-a-word puzzles. They've been lying around for a couple weeks.

CLAIRE. Oh, I love search-a-word puzzles! *(Beat.)* Don't I?

RICHARD. Yes, but they just lie there.

CLAIRE. Hand me one. I'll do one right now. Watch. *(Takes search-a-word book.)*

RICHARD. Did I tell you I've been taking a self-defense class at the Y? Last night we learned how to disarm a mugger. It's all in the wrist. You grab them here — *(Demonstrates on his wrist.)*

CLAIRE. *(Still in search-a-word.)* Oh, I just found "kumquat"! *(Kenny reenters and goes to Claire's purse.)*

KENNY. I need some money for the bus.

RICHARD. Let's show your mother how to disarm a mugger.

KENNY. I'm taking a twenty. *(Rummages through purse for money.)*

RICHARD. Oh no you don't. *(Lunges at him with large deliberate moves on each "no!")* No! No! No! *(Twists Kenny's wrist hard.)*

KENNY. Ow! What the hell are you doing?!

RICHARD. Impressive, eh?

KENNY. You could've busted my wrist, ass-wipe! *(Picks money off floor.)*

RICHARD. You don't need that much money for the bus.

KENNY. Quit riding me.

RICHARD. It's chilly. Put on your blue sweater.

KENNY. *(To Richard.)* Why can't you just die?! *(Exits.)*

CLAIRE. *(Nose in search-a-word.)* Here's "kiwi"! It's a fruit-themed puzzle!

RICHARD. He's gonna buy drugs with that money.

CLAIRE. What grade is he in?

RICHARD. Eighth.

CLAIRE. My goodness. He's big for middle school.

RICHARD. He's dyslexic. We're hoping he finally graduates this year.

CLAIRE. *(Puts down search-a-word.)* I'm not sure what's going on exactly.

RICHARD. No, I know. I'm sorry, honey. *(Sits next to her.)* Uh … It's like this: My name is Richard Fiffle, and I'm your husband.

CLAIRE. You are? My goodness.

RICHARD. Don't be alarmed.

CLAIRE. Who's the boy?

RICHARD. That's your son.

CLAIRE. Really? How much did he weigh at birth?

RICHARD. I don't know, but he loves you very much.

CLAIRE. He's so angry.

RICHARD. He's having a difficult time right now.

CLAIRE. Have I been in a coma of some kind?

RICHARD. No. You have a form of psychogenic amnesia.

CLAIRE. Oh dear, that sounds gruesome. Do go on.

RICHARD.   Well, two years ago you woke up one day and your memory was completely gone.

CLAIRE.   How strange.

RICHARD.   The doctors assumed it was temporary, but now they're not so sure.

CLAIRE.   Doctors aren't very smart are they?

RICHARD.   No, they're not. The strange thing is you're usually very lucid and capable of understanding complex thoughts. You even retain an enormous amount of information in the course of the day, but as soon as you go to sleep, it's gone. The next morning we have to start all over again.

CLAIRE.   That must be very annoying for you.

RICHARD.   Yes, it is.

CLAIRE.   So every morning we have the same conversation?

RICHARD.   Yes. Well, I change a word here and there, but mostly it's the same. Sometimes I don't admit it's annoying.

CLAIRE.   That's very sweet of you … sometimes.

RICHARD.   *(Grabs what looks like a large Filofax from side table and hands it to her.)* This is a book I designed to get you through your day. I worked very hard on it. *(Turns pages.)* See, here's a layout of the house. How the appliances work. Little photos and descriptions of people you may meet.

CLAIRE.   Oh, who is that pathetically sad-looking woman?

RICHARD.   That's you, darling.

CLAIRE.   No, it can't be! Get me a mirror.

RICHARD.   It's an old photo. *(Hands her a mirror.)* Before you lost your memory.

CLAIRE.   *(Looks at herself in the mirror.)* Oh, yes. I look much happier now, Philip.

RICHARD.   Richard.

CLAIRE.   Right. This photo's too gloomy. Let's get something more chipper.

RICHARD.   All right.

CLAIRE.   Tell me, *Richard*, if my memory serves me correctly — *(Stops and laughs at herself.)* Aren't I being ironic?

RICHARD.   You make that joke every day.

CLAIRE.   Hm. Do you ever laugh?

RICHARD.   No.

8

CLAIRE.   How sad. Anyway, if my memory serves me correctly, isn't amnesia usually brought on by some sort of physical or psychological trauma?

RICHARD.   *(Beat.)* Uh … I'm not sure what you mean.

CLAIRE.   I mean something horrible happens and then amnesia kicks in. Yes, I believe that's correct. I don't know why I remember that.

RICHARD.   I need to hop into the shower.

CLAIRE.   I don't usually mention trauma, do I?

RICHARD.   No. Actually you've *never* mentioned it.

CLAIRE.   I could tell by your face that I hadn't. Oh, today *is* a special day, isn't it?

RICHARD.   I'll be in the shower for a little while. I need to be at the hospital for a few hours today.

CLAIRE.   But what happened to me?

RICHARD.   Small steps, darling. We don't want to exhaust you so early in the morning.

CLAIRE.   Oh, I bet it was unbearable!

RICHARD.   The fridge is full. Help yourself.

CLAIRE.   Thanks.

RICHARD.   Love you.

CLAIRE.   Uh … okay. *(Richard smiles and exits. Claire calls after him.)* Hey, what's my name? *(No response.)* Richard? *(But he's gone.)* So, I have amnesia. Hm, that's very inconvenient. *(Beat.)* I wonder if I always talk to myself. *(Opens the book and reads.)* "Good morning, Claire." Claire. Claire. Apparently my name is Claire. *(Reads book again.)* "I'm sorry you have no memory." Oh that's very sweet. "To begin your day, put on your slippers. They are located beside the bed." *(She sees the slippers.)* Oh, so they are. This is so clever. It's like a little scavenger hunt. *(Puts slippers on, then reads.)* "Second, take a deep breath and greet the morning." *(She does.)* Hello, Morning! *(The head of a man in a ski mask pops out from under the bed.)*

LIMPING MAN.   Hello, Claire.

CLAIRE.   Oh my. *(The man in the ski-mask crawls out from under the bed. He walks with a limp and speaks with a lisp.)*

LIMPING MAN.   Sshhhhh. Don't thay anything.

CLAIRE.   Oh dear.

LIMPING MAN.   Pleathe, don't be sthcared. I'm thaving you.

CLAIRE.   All right. *(The man has a manacle on one wrist, a bit of chain hanging down as if it's been cut.)*

LIMPING MAN.   You have to come with me.

CLAIRE.   *(Flipping through book.)* Hold on, I haven't reached this part yet.

LIMPING MAN.   Claire, quickly. While he'th in the shower.

CLAIRE.   I'm sorry, this is a little confusing for me.

LIMPING MAN.   I'm here to thave you.

CLAIRE.   *(Still with book.)* But it doesn't say anything in here about a limping man in a ski mask.

LIMPING MAN.   Pleathe, Claire. If you ever loved me, then come with me now.

CLAIRE.   Do I know you?

LIMPING MAN.   It'th me. Thachary. Your brother. Thachary. Thack! Thacky!

CLAIRE.   I have a brother?

LIMPING MAN.   Yeth, Claire. Now pleathe, leth sthkedaddle.

CLAIRE.   You have such a pronounced lisp.

LIMPING MAN.   Yeth, and I altho can't walk properly. I'll exthplain everything later. We've gotta go.

CLAIRE.   But I'm in my pajamas.

LIMPING MAN.   *(Grabs dress and some shoes.)* That man in the shower ith going to kill you, Claire. He'th a very dangeruth perthon.

CLAIRE.   But he seemed so nice.

LIMPING MAN.   Leth go, Claire. Pleathe. Come with me.

CLAIRE.   Are you gonna take off that mask?

LIMPING MAN.   There'th no time.

CLAIRE.   Can I take my search-a-word?

LIMPING MAN.   Yeth but for godthaykth leth go!

CLAIRE.   *(Grabs puzzle book and Filofax.)* This is very strange. You do know I have no memory to speak of?

LIMPING MAN.   *(Rushes her out.)* Leth be sthpeedy, Claire. Sthpeedy sthpeedy ethcape. You'll thank me later. *(Lights down on the bedroom. Sounds of cars on a road transition us into —)*

SCENE 2

Lights up in the Limping Man's car. He's driving. Claire sits beside him.

LIMPING MAN.   Tho, here we are. Thack and hith thithter. Ith been thuch a long time, Claire.

CLAIRE.   Has it?

LIMPING MAN.   Ith very thad whath happened to you.

CLAIRE.   Are you gonna take off that mask now?

LIMPING MAN.   If you inthitht. But pleathe, don't be thcared.

CLAIRE.   Are you deformed?

LIMPING MAN.   Yeth. Yeth I am. But only thlightly.

CLAIRE.   Ooo, an *unveiling*. I can't wait to see what — *(He pulls off his mask. His right ear is a twisted mass of burnt scar tissue.)* Ewwwww, your ear is a twisted mass of burnt scar tissue.

LIMPING MAN.   Pleathe, try to be a little thenthitive.

CLAIRE.   You limp, you lisp and your ear is all clumpy. What happened to you?

LIMPING MAN.   Claire, do you really not remember?

CLAIRE.   I'm sorry, I don't.

LIMPING MAN.   Good. Ith better you didn't. Thum things are better left forgotten.

CLAIRE.   I don't know if that's true.

LIMPING MAN.   What?

CLAIRE.   I don't know if that's true.

LIMPING MAN.   You don't know if *whath* blue?

CLAIRE.   *True*, I said!

LIMPING MAN.   Oh. I'm thorry, but whenever you thit on my right like thith, you'll have to thpeak up. I'm deaf in thith ear.

CLAIRE.   *(Yelling into his clumpy ear.)* All right!

LIMPING MAN.   I'm altho blind in thith eye.

CLAIRE.   Should you be driving?

LIMPING MAN.   No, but tho long ath they don't catch me,

11

we'll be thuper.

CLAIRE.   So long as who doesn't catch you?

LIMPING MAN.   Pleathe, you're athking too many quethtions.

CLAIRE.   I'm sorry, but that's all I have right now.

LIMPING MAN.   Juth look out for the right thide of the car.

CLAIRE.   Where are we going again?

LIMPING MAN.   To the country. Your mother hath a houth there.

CLAIRE.   She does?

LIMPING MAN.   *Our* mother I mean. She'th my mother too, even if she tethtified againtht me, even if she thaid I wath dead to her, she'th thtill my mother.

CLAIRE.   Is she nice?

LIMPING MAN.   She had a thtroke rethently and hath trouble forming thententheth properly.

CLAIRE.   We're quite a family it seems.

LIMPING MAN.   Yeth. Yeth we are.

CLAIRE.   *(Flips through her book.)* Does it say anything in here about her?

LIMPING MAN.   Put that book away.

CLAIRE.   *(Removes photo from book.)* Oh look, here's a photo. "Gertie's House" it says. Mama's name is Gertie, isn't it? Yes, this house is very familiar. And is that sweet-looking lady Gertie?

LIMPING MAN.   *(Grabs book.)* Don't believe anything in thith book, Claire. Ith all lithe. Lithe that that man made up. Ith garbage. *(Throws it out the car window.)*

CLAIRE.   Hey, I needed that book.

LIMPING MAN.   You have me now, and I'll tell you everything you need to know.

CLAIRE.   All right then, how did I lose my memory?

LIMPING MAN.   Exthept that. Your memory problem and the thtory of my phythical infirmiteeth are the two thingth I can't talk about.

CLAIRE.   Why are you taking me away like this?

LIMPING MAN.   Okay, three thingth, but thath not tho much.

CLAIRE.   And why is there a manacle on your wrist?

LIMPING MAN.   *(Getting annoyed.)* All right, tho there are

12

many thingth I can't thay right now, but in time everything will be exthplained! *(We hear echoey carnival music far off.)*

CLAIRE.   Is that your radio playing?

LIMPING MAN.   The radio'th buthted.

CLAIRE.   Where's that music coming from then?

LIMPING MAN.   I don't hear no muthic.

CLAIRE.   Ooo, it must be a side effect of the amnesia. Fun. It's kinda catchy. *(Claire hums along to the music, then notices something in the rearview mirror.)* Oh, look at that. I have a little scar on my forehead. How'd I get that, Zack? *(A very loud horn blares suddenly.)* Trailer changing lanes! Trailer changing lanes!

LIMPING MAN.	CLAIRE.
(Looking around madly.)	*(Pointing frantically.)*
Where?! Where?!	There! There!

(He swerves the car. We hear a screech. The trailer horn fades off.)

LIMPING MAN.   Thank you.

CLAIRE.   Maybe *I* should drive.

LIMPING MAN.   No, I'm good. We'll be there in no time. Juth relaxth.

CLAIRE.   I'm not sure I can at this point, Zack. But I'll try.

(Puts photo in her pocket. The lights fade on Limping Man driving, and a concerned Claire looking around. Again, sounds of cars transition us into —)

SCENE 3

Lights up on Gertie's kitchen. She's in her sixties, wears a bathrobe and is sipping tea. Claire appears in the kitchen window, looking in at Gertie. She holds up the photo and looks at it, then at Gertie, making sure they're the same.

CLAIRE. *(At window.)* Mama?! You're Mama, right? Mama, it's me. Your daughter Claire. I have amnesia.

GERTIE. Clay? Whadda dune hay? Youshen be gnome!

CLAIRE. I hear you've had a stroke. That's terrible.

GERTIE. Income, Clay. Income!

CLAIRE. Did you know I was traumatized and no one will tell me what happened?

GERTIE. *(Waving her in.)* Income, Clay. In … come … in … come in.

CLAIRE. Oh, all right. *(The Limping Man appears at the window. Gertie's surprised and unhappy to see him.)*

LIMPING MAN. Hello, Mama. Did you mith me?

CLAIRE. Look, Mama, it's Zack! Are you surprised? I was too. But he was wearing a mask when I saw him, so it was surprising *and* scary at the same time.

GERTIE. *(To Limping Man.)* Fee, whadda helen oodoo?

CLAIRE. He's apparently saving me from Richard Fiffle.

LIMPING MAN. I know you're not happy to thee me.

GERTIE. Dashen dunder-mince-tate.

CLAIRE. Zack was saying you two didn't get along.

LIMPING MAN. But I'm juth thtaying a couple hourth, Mama, and I'll be on my betht behavior if you thtay on yourth. Okay?

GERTIE. Income, Clay.

CLAIRE. *(To Limping Man.)* That means *"come in"* in stroke talk.

LIMPING MAN. We'll come around the front. I remember the

14

way.

CLAIRE.   See ya in a sec! *(Claire and Limping Man leave window and go around front. Gertie collects herself. She grabs a knife from a drawer, places it within reach, and throws a dish towel over it to hide it. Limping Man and Claire enter the kitchen. Claire, happy to see her mother:)* Mama!

GERTIE.   Clay! *(Hugs Claire.)*

LIMPING MAN.   Jeeth Loueeth, thith kitchen hathn't changed a bit. Ith like a mutheum.

CLAIRE.   I think it's a pretty house. I can tell I grew up here.

LIMPING MAN.   *(Grabs dusty old baseball mitt from top of fridge.)* Hey, my old baseball glove!

CLAIRE.   I feel like I've come home to the bosom of my mama.

LIMPING MAN.   You know what I like about it? The theclusion. Privathy ith pritheleth.

CLAIRE.   *(Looks out the window.)* What a huge tree. *(To Limping Man.)* Did you climb it?

LIMPING MAN.   What?

CLAIRE.   When you were little? You used to climb that tree all the time. Right? Higher and higher?

LIMPING MAN.   *(Beat.)* Yeah. I did. Right, Gertie?

CLAIRE.   See? I remember some things. Don't tell me I don't remember things.

GERTIE.   Fast break?

CLAIRE.   What?

GERTIE.   Fast break, Clay? Eggs? Sear-el? Toe-sat? Fast break?

CLAIRE.   Breakfast?

GERTIE.   Fast break, Clay?

CLAIRE.   I'd love some. We just ran out this morning and didn't have any time to stop and eat. *(Gertie opens up the freezer door.)*

GERTIE.   Balcony?

CLAIRE.   No, I don't think I want baloney, Mama.

GERTIE.   *(Holds up bacon.)* Balcony?

LIMPING MAN.   No! Goddamnit, no bacon! Never bacon! Never make bacon! *(Throws bacon out the window.)* You *know* I don't like bacon, Gertie.

CLAIRE.   *(Pause.)* I think you should apologize. You scared

Mama.

LIMPING MAN.   I'm thorry. I don't … like … bacon.

GERTIE.   I jez hava fidful oh da balcony cuz ya foddeh lie dit so moo. I jez godden haboo oh keeboo da-roun oda tie.

CLAIRE.   Hmmm. That's a very good story, Mama.

LIMPING MAN.   You have a hackthaw, Mom?

GERTIE.   Hack?

LIMPING MAN.   Yeah, I have thomething to do.

GERTIE.   Ina la.

LIMPING MAN.   What?

GERTIE.   La.

LIMPING MAN.   La?

CLAIRE.   In the cellar, she said. Daddy's workbench is against the back wall. And there are some saws hanging to the left. There's a hacksaw with a red handle.

LIMPING MAN.   *(Beat.)* Thankth, Claire. *(Exits into basement.)*

CLAIRE.   This house is so nice, Mama. I know things about it. It's good for me, right?

GERTIE.   Clay …

CLAIRE.   Did they tell you I lose my memory every day? That must be a very rare thing. *(Inhales deeply.)* Oh I think I can still smell Daddy's cologne. It must've seeped into the wallpaper.

GERTIE.   I doan tinktoe, Clay. *(Checks that Limping Man's out of earshot.)*

CLAIRE.   *(Straining to remember.)* Yes, I think I can picture him. Did he wear a yellow cap?

GERTIE.   Clay, lessco fo wah, kay?

CLAIRE.   Hold on. There used to be cages out back, weren't there? With dogs in them. And Daddy would feed them in the morning.

GERTIE.   Isso ny ow sigh, lessco fo wah.

CLAIRE.   He'd line up all those dog dishes and fill them with kibble, and I'd help him carry them out to the cages. You and Dad ran a kennel.

GERTIE.   Ya, da kenny. Buh Clay, lissa toe-me, peas.

CLAIRE.   And Daddy would walk all the dogs at once. Seven or eight at a time. All these leashes pulling in different directions.

And he'd come over that hill looking like a map of the universe. Yeah, Daddy's yellow hat was the sun and he had all these dog planets revolving around him. And on the longest leash was Mrs. Paulson's terrier Chippy. And Chippy was like the planet Pluto, because he was so far away from Daddy and so little. How long ago was that, Mama? I must've been about ten. *(A homemade handpuppet, equipped with little arms in little manacles, appears in the window.)*

MILLET. *(As puppet, in a goofy voice.)* Hellooooo beautiful ladies. My name is Hinky Binky. Can I be your friend?

CLAIRE. *(Beat.)* Well this is very strange, isn't it?

MILLET. *(As puppet.)* I've got an itch on the top of my head that I can't reach. It's driving me craaaaaazyyy!

CLAIRE. Who are you?

MILLET. *(As puppet.)* I'm Hinky Binky. Scratch my head.

CLAIRE. Is this normal, Mama?

MILLET. *(As puppet.)* Scratch my itch, bitch!

CLAIRE. Excuse me, but you're not being very nice.

PUPPET. Nice bites, right Millet? *(His normal voice.)* Don't say my name. *(Puppet voice.)* Why can't I say your name, *Millet?* *(Normal.)* You're gonna get me in trouble! *(Puppet singing.)* Miiiiilllllleeeeettttttt ... Milllleeeettttttt. *(A grizzled man stands up, the puppet on his hand. He strangles the puppet.)* Cut it out! You gotta remember the rules! *(Realizes that he's been seen.)* AHH! *(Claire and Gertie scream when he screams. He disappears again.)*

CLAIRE. What a crazy puppet man. Do you know him, Mama?

GERTIE. No, Clay. Ida know no puppas! *(Limping Man runs in with hacksaw.)*

LIMPING MAN. Wath that Millet?

CLAIRE. You know him?

LIMPING MAN. Where'd he go?

CLAIRE. He scared us. *(The puppet appears again at the window.)*

MILLET. *(As puppet.)* I'm Hinky Binky with the two-foot dinky.

CLAIRE. What a filthy puppet.

LIMPING MAN. Millet! *(Limping Man grabs puppet and pulls it off the Millet's hand, revealing that Millet too has a manacle on his*

17

wrist.)

MILLET. *(Still with puppet voice.)* Yikes, now I'm just a hand. Boo hoo hoo!

LIMPING MAN. I thought we talked about thith? *(Millet stands in window, shame-faced.)*

MILLET. I'm sorry.

LIMPING MAN. Didn't we talk about thith?

MILLET. Yes. Can I have my puppet back?

LIMPING MAN. You frightened the women.

MILLET. I'm real sorry, ladies.

LIMPING MAN. He didn't mean nothing by it. Milleth okay. *(Hands him puppet.)*

MILLET. Thank you. *(Puts it back on.)* I feel much better.

LIMPING MAN. Thith ith Claire.

MILLET. Nice to meet you, ma'am.

LIMPING MAN. And thath Gertie.

MILLET. *(As puppet.)* Like a hurdy-gurdy? If I turn your crank will you play? *(Millet and Limping Man laugh at the puppet's strange joke.)*

CLAIRE. You both have manacles on. Did you escape from a chain gang? *(They stop laughing.)*

LIMPING MAN. You should juth know, Claire, that everything I do, I do for you.

MILLET. We gonna cut this cuff off? *(As puppet.)* Please cut it off. I'm gonna go craaaaazyyy.

LIMPING MAN. We got a vithe in the bathement. That'll hold 'em in plathe. You come around the front.

MILLET. *(As puppet.)* I'll be there in two shakes! *(Goes around front.)*

LIMPING MAN. Now you both be nithe to Millet. Hith mother wath a freebather.

CLAIRE. A what?

LIMPING MAN. A *free*bather. *(Claire still doesn't get it.)*

GERTIE. A base-freezer, Clay. Day base-freeze croquet.

CLAIRE. Oh. I love croquet. I was always the blue mallet. *(Claire laughs; those were good times. Now it's Gertie and Limping Man who are confused. Millet strolls in, wearing a stolen suit with the price tags and security tags still attached.)*

MILLET. Sorry I'm late. I stopped by J.C. Penney to pick this up. *(Indicates suit, then notices the kitchen.)* Wow, this is so weird. Because one time — *(Cheery puppet.)* Millet was sodomized in a house like this.

LIMPING MAN. Hey!

MILLET. Sorry. He's not used to being around ladies.

LIMPING MAN. Did you get everything on the list?

MILLET. Yeah, it's all in the trunk of my car.

CLAIRE. Did you steal those cars?

MILLET. Yeah, we did!

LIMPING MAN. Millet —

MILLET. *(Realizes.)* Oh, I mean … we made them.

CLAIRE. And the manacles … You guys used to be attached?

MILLET. Yeah. They chain us together when we work in the kitchen.

LIMPING MAN. What I thay about talking?

MILLET. Oops. You said don't say too much at the *rendezvous.*

CLAIRE. This is a rendezvous?

LIMPING MAN. *(To Millet.)* You thee what happent? More quethtionth.

MILLET. I won't say anything else.

LIMPING MAN. Now leth go to the bathement.

MILLET. *(Sings as puppet.)* And then we'll shuffle off to Buffalo.
(Limping Man and Millet exit into basement.)

CLAIRE. Life can be so funny, Mama.

GERTIE. Clay, noo-noo dish is gooey.

CLAIRE. What's the matter?

GERTIE. Ees med ah noose bah.

CLAIRE. We need a dictionary for you. A translation book.

GERTIE. Clay, dish is nah — *(Limping Man re-enters.)*

LIMPING MAN. Claire, come talk to me and Millet in the bathement. I haven't theen you in tho long. You can talk to Mama any old time.

CLAIRE. That puppet's got a potty mouth, Philip.

LIMPING MAN. Thack.

CLAIRE. Right. Zack. What'd I say?

LIMPING MAN. I'll tell him to thtop with the puppet. Milleth not too bright, but he lithenth.

CLAIRE.   All right then. Mama, do you mind? I've never spent any time with criminals before.

LIMPING MAN.   You know that for thertain, Claire? *(Laughs at his joke.)*

CLAIRE.   Oh, right. I get it. I lost my memory so —

LIMPING MAN.   We'll be doing handiwork, Gertie. *(Limping Man and Claire go to basement. Gertie goes to the phone and dials 911.)*

GERTIE.   *(Into phone.)* Isis Geht Maso. Fee cape. Eesh ina hiss … Huh? … *(They don't understand her, she clarifies.)* Fee cape … Cape … Ee brogue adder summer … *Fee Cape!* … Geht Maso! … *Fee cape!!!* (Limping Man reenters. He forgot something. Gertie quickly tries to look like she's making small talk. Into phone:)* Ish da rye? Dah isho fuddy.

LIMPING MAN.   Who are you talking to, Gertie?

GERTIE.   *(Into phone.)* Hoe-down do sicken. *(To Limping Man.)* Iyas mah frient … I cull mah frient … thall.

LIMPING MAN.   *(Hangs the phone up.)* How 'bout we keep quiet? No calling people. No blabbing to Claire. Juth quiet time, okay?

GERTIE.   No Fee, yoda ony baddy doo Clay.

LIMPING MAN.   You mention anything and I'll kill you, Gertie. I thwear to God, I'll cut off your fuckin' head and *bury you in THE BACK YARD!!! (Silence.)* I'm thorry. You juth … Leth be normal, okay? *(Apologetically.)* Really, I'm trying to … You want thum candy? *(Pulls candy from pockets and lays it on table.)* Here, have thum candy. Thee? I can be good, Mama. Watch. I'll juth thit here and be good while you make breakfatht. Like in the old dayth. They don't need me down there. I can be good, Mama. I *can* be. *(Lights down on the kitchen. The sound of someone scanning a car radio transitions us into —)*

SCENE 4

Lights up inside car. Richard drives. Kenny is smoking a joint and scanning the car radio.

RICHARD.   Kenny, can you please just pick a station and stay there? *(Kenny stops on a '70s easy-listening song.)*
KENNY.   Sweet. *(Leans back and takes a hit from his joint.)*
RICHARD.   You know, most fathers wouldn't allow their kids to smoke marijuana in the car. I hope you appreciate how understanding I'm trying to be.
KENNY.   Why did you pick me up at the bus stop? I said I didn't need a ride. *(Richard clicks off the radio.)* Hey, I was listening to that.
RICHARD.   Kenny, listen to me. Your mother is missing.
KENNY.   Huh. *(Takes another hit.)*
RICHARD.   You gotta help me be the search party. Keep your eyes open, she could be anywhere. *(Kenny exhales pot smoke.)* Hey, blow it that way. I'm getting a contact buzz.
KENNY.   So wait, she just wandered off?
RICHARD.   She was acting a little strange this morning.
KENNY.   Maybe she finally wised up and ran away from your nutty ass.
RICHARD.   I love your mother, Kenny. Very much. I know you harbor some animosity for me, but I've tried to be a good husband and a good father, and if I've misplaced your mother, I've lost everything.
KENNY.   You know what I hear when you talk? "Kenny, blah-blah-bloopity-bloop."
RICHARD.   I can tell you're upset. Well, you know what? Don't even think of this as a search party. Just think of it as a drive in the car. This is what families do. They go for drives. You wanna play "I Spy"?

KENNY.   Are you retarded?

RICHARD.   Okay, I'm hearing that you're angry. And the pot tells me you're trying to dull the pain at the center of your life.

KENNY.   *(Snickers.)* The road is all wobbly.

RICHARD.   But I know the siren call of ganja, Kenny. They used to call me Maryjane McGee. Or Cannabis Carl. Or J.P. Toke-Meister.

KENNY.   *(Staring intently at his hand.)* Hands can look like spiders.

RICHARD.   But it leads to other things. Terrible, damaging things. I know. I used to have a very serious drug problem. You should learn from my mistakes like other children.

KENNY.   Other children learn from your mistakes?

RICHARD.   What? You're stoned. *(Beat.)* Wanna play "I Went on a Picnic"?

KENNY.   I bet if I had bionic eyes we could find her really quick.

RICHARD.   I think she's hitchhiking to your grandmother's.

KENNY.   Why do you think that?

RICHARD.   *(Holds up her book.)* I found her book on the road and the only thing missing from it is the photo of Gertie's house.

KENNY.   Weird. *(Looks out the window.)* Oh my god, that van-load of kids is staring at me. Look at them. They're all staring right through me. It's wiggin' me out.

RICHARD.   Ah yes, the paranoia. For a long time I thought there were people after me too. But that's because I did something very bad, and I've never paid for it, so I was always waiting for the other foot to drop. But it never did. And I pray it never will. *(Silence as Kenny stares at him.)* I'm sorry. I'm feeling a little off-kilter today. I hope we find your mother soon. Otherwise I — I don't what I'm gonna — may I have a hit?

KENNY.   What?

RICHARD.   Just a little one. To take the edge off. *(Kenny passes him the joint. Richard takes a hit. Holding breath in:)* I really shouldn't be doing this but I'm worried about your mom and — *(Suddenly.)* Did I ever tell you about the time I met Dennis Hopper? *(A siren blares in distance.)* Aw geez, it's the fuzz. *(Tosses joint out the window.)* Open the windows. Air it out. *(Pulls over.)*

See what happens, Kenny? Drugs lead to crime. Let that be a lesson. Try and act natural. *(Waits for cop.)* Jeepers. I get awful jumpy around the pigs. How are my eyes? Bloodshot?

KENNY.   Shut up, moron. *(Heidi, a cop, approaches.)*

RICHARD.   How-do, officer?

HEIDI.   In a hurry this morning?

RICHARD.   Not especially. I'm just out for a drive with the boy, playing some "I Spy," heading to the Friendly's for a treat.

HEIDI.   Kinda early for a Fribble, isn't it?

RICHARD.   Not for this family. We love ice cream. Right, Kenny?

HEIDI.   I clocked you going 84 in a 55 zone.

RICHARD.   Is that right? Well, I'll be. Maybe that speedy-radar thingy of yours needs new batteries. *(Kenny gets a giggle-fit which may last through the scene.)*

HEIDI.   Have you been smoking marijuana in this vehicle, sir?

RICHARD.   No ma'am I have not.

HEIDI.   Smells like maybe someone was, sir.

RICHARD.   Well, Kenny here, I must admit was toking up a bit of the doobage, so to speak.

HEIDI.   I'll be needing your license and registration, sir, and then I'd like you both to step out of the vehicle.

RICHARD.   Oh, you misunderstood me. You see, Kenny here has glaucoma and he smokes pot for purely medicinal purposes.

HEIDI.   And do you have a letter from your doctor stating as much?

RICHARD.   Actually, our doctor had a terrible accident and he no longer has hands, so writing a note isn't possible for him right now. But as soon as he's fitted for prosthetic limbs and learns how to write with those awkward little hooks I'll pass the note onto the Highway Patrol Office.

HEIDI.   I believe you're lying to me, sir.

RICHARD.   No, he was fiddling inside a lawn mower in between operations and —

HEIDI.   Sir?

RICHARD.   All right, I'm lying. But Kenny here is a troubled teen and — Fritos! I suddenly want Fritos! Are you craving Fritos, Kenny? *(Snickers.)*

KENNY.   Mmmmm. Fritos.

HEIDI. *(Pulls gun on him.)* Please step out of the vehicle, sir!

RICHARD. Hold on there, flatfoot. I don't think we need you pulling a Rodney King here.

HEIDI. Get out of the car!

RICHARD. Okay. We're getting out, but this is all much ado about nothing, eh Kenny? *(They step out of car, Heidi's gun on them. Kenny is trying not to giggle.)*

HEIDI. License and registration please.

RICHARD. *(Hands them over.)* This is all very unnecessary, officer. You see, my wife has a form of psychogenic amnesia and she wandered off this morning ...

HEIDI. I think I've heard just about enough of your stories, tough guy.

RICHARD. Tough guy? I'm not tough guy. I'm *nice* guy. Everyone I know calls me *nice* guy.

HEIDI. *(Looking at license.)* Well, Mr. *Fiffle*, if that's your *real* name, I'm gonna radio back to headquarters and have them pop your name into a computer and see what turns up.

RICHARD. Headquarters? Computer? No! No! No! *(He goes into self-defense mode, lunging at her with each "no!" He twists her wrist so she drops the gun. He scrambles for it and points it at her.)* Well, the shoe's on the other hand now, isn't it, copper?

HEIDI. Sir, I am a police officer, which means you need to return my revolver.

RICHARD. I'm sorry, but that isn't possible. You see, I have a very complicated past and can't afford your popping my name into any computer. So I'm afraid you're gonna have to come with us.

KENNY. You're gonna get us thrown in jail, shit-for-brains.

RICHARD. You know what, Kenny? I wish you'd stop calling me names. It hurts my feelings.

HEIDI. Sir, why don't you just head on home, I'll forget I stopped you and we'll call it a day.

RICHARD. Because I have to find my wife! It's only been a couple hours and look at me!

HEIDI. Sir, let's not get excited.

RICHARD. Everyone back in the car! *(Lights out on them. The '70s easy-listening song transitions us into —)*

SCENE 5

The basement of Gertie's house. There's a workbench with a vice nearby, as well as several boxes filled with old toys and junk. Millet's manacle has been cut off and sits on the workbench with a few old dolls. As the lights come up, Claire is jumping rope. Millet is trying to hula hoop. They sing a children's song together. Millet sings as the puppet.

CLAIRE and MILLET.   Cinderella, dressed in yella.
    Went downstairs to kiss a fella.
    Made a mistake and kissed a snake.
    How many doctors did it take?
    One. Two. Three. Four —
(Claire messes up and stops skipping rope. Millet stops hula hooping.)
MILLET.   *(Puppet.)* Four! It took four doctors! *(They laugh together, giddy.)*
CLAIRE.   Isn't it fun down here?
MILLET.   Yeah. *(Suddenly notices a nearby kewpie doll.)* Except for that doll. It's kinda creepy. Face it the other way, okay?
CLAIRE.   *(Picks up kewpie doll.)* Oh, look at that. I bet someone won it for me. I bet my dad knocked down a stack of milk bottles with one shot! Whaddaya think?
MILLET.   I think maybe you weren't supposed to go through that stuff.
CLAIRE.   Why?
MILLET.   I ... I should tell Zack I cut off my manacle. *(Heads for stairs.)*
CLAIRE.   *(Cuts him off at the pass.)* Hold on, Millet. He's busy making up with Mama.
MILLET.   Yeah, but I don't like basements.
CLAIRE.   Oh come on, we're having so much fun.
MILLET.   *(Puppet.)* And you didn't cut off *my* manacles! *(Normal.)* But Binky — *(Puppet.)* I'm gettin' all squirrelly! Now

cut 'em off! *(Normal.)* Okay! Stop yelling! *(To Claire.)* Binky's got little manacles too.

CLAIRE.   Yeah. I saw that. Cute.

MILLET.   Thanks. *(Millet puts Binky's tiny manacle in the vise and begins sawing them off.)*

CLAIRE.   Do you think they're talking about me up there?

MILLET.   I … I don't know.

CLAIRE.   Sure you don't know. *(Pulls monster mask from box.)* Look. I bet it was Zack's. I bet he'd wear it and scare me and make me scream. *(Laughs at mask.)*

MILLET.   It gives me the willies. Put it away, okay?

CLAIRE.   You're such a Nervous Nellie.

MILLET.   Hey, where'd you get that ring?

CLAIRE.   *(Notices it for the first time.)* Oh. I don't know.

MILLET.   Principal Leone had a ring just like that.

CLAIRE.   Who's Principal Leone?

MILLET.   My old boss. I used to be janitor at a grade school.

CLAIRE.   Is that right?

MILLET.   And Principal Leone had a ring just like that. Hers had a nice diamond in the middle and two rubies on the side. Every morning I would say, "Hello Principal Leone. That's a very pretty ring." *(Puppet.)* Stupid whore wrecked your life! *(Normal.)* She fired me.

CLAIRE.   Why'd she do that?

MILLET.   Oh, I … I'm not supposed to —

CLAIRE.   Come on, you can talk about *yourself.* He just told you to not say anything about *me*, right?

MILLET.   She … she said I scared the children. I would growl at them and chase them with my pail of sawdust for fun. And she said I scared the children.

CLAIRE.   I'm sorry, Millet.

MILLET.   And the next day, when I woke up, there were two cops standing over my bed. And they said I beat up Principal Leone in the parking lot and stole her ring. Which was very surprising to me. I mean, in court I had to admit that I had just been fired, and yes I had said I liked her ring, and it was true that often I have blackouts, but I'm not a violent person.

CLAIRE.   So, that's how you ended up in prison? You stole a ring?

MILLET.   I guess so.

CLAIRE.   And that's where you met Zack?

MILLET.   Yeah, in the yard.

CLAIRE.   Oh, the *yard*. It sounds so rough. Was he lifting weights?

MILLET.   No. This lifer named Twitchy was threatening Binky with a shiv. *(Puppet.)* So I squeezed his nuts and made him cry! *(Normal.)* But then the guards started shooting at us from the towers, and Zack pushed us out of the way of the bullets. So we became friends. He likes to talk to me.

CLAIRE.   Oh yeah? Does he ever say anything about me?

MILLET.   Sure. He calls you his little blank thlate.

CLAIRE.   Really? Does he ever say *why* I'm his little blank thlate?

MILLET.   Uhh ... I'm not really allowed to talk about it.

CLAIRE.   Oh, right.

MILLET.   It's just ... he has these plans —

CLAIRE.   Plans?

MILLET.   And he made me promise not to say too much, which is hard for me, because when I get nervous, I just jabber on.

CLAIRE.   Why are you nervous?

MILLET.   *(As puppet.)* Millet's a chicken-shit! *(Laughs at Binky.)* I just don't like basements. *(As puppet.)* Plus *I've* got a biiiiiiiggggg mouth! *(Normal.)* Yeah, I'm a little afraid of Binky getting me in trouble.

CLAIRE.   Well, he hasn't said anything too damaging yet.

MILLET.   *(As puppet.)* Give it time, bitch!

CLAIRE.   I wish he didn't have such a foul mouth.

MILLET.   Yeah, me too.

CLAIRE.   Where'd you get him anyway?

MILLET.   I made him. A lady from the church came into the prison and showed us how. *(Puppet.)* Fuckin' nuns, I hate them! *(Normal.)* Sorry. Catholic school.

CLAIRE.   Oh, you're Catholic.

MILLET.   Not me. Just Binky.

CLAIRE.   Oh. *(Pulls squirt gun from box.)* Look, squirt gun! It's so funny, Gertie saved all our toys. *(As Claire holds up the squirt gun, we hear a dog barking, far off, echoey. She looks around, disoriented.)* Did you hear that?

MILLET.   What?

CLAIRE.   The dog. You didn't hear a dog barking? *(Taps her head with the palm of her hand.)*

MILLET.   No. You okay?

CLAIRE.   Yeah, I just … I'm fine. *(Claire puts the squirt gun down. Millet returns to sawing his cuff.)* I'd tell *you*, you know.

MILLET.   What?

CLAIRE.   If I knew what happened during those blackouts of yours and you wanted to know, I'd tell you.

MILLET.   I can't. I'm just here to saw my manacle. I'm sorry.

CLAIRE.   *(Playful.)* Oh. You're sorry? *(Puts on mask, silly monster voice.)* Millet's sorry he can't talk about Claire's amnesia. *(Millet laughs nervously. Claire creeps to him. Monster voice:)* Well, what if I *made* you talk about it? *(Points squirt gun at him.)*

MILLET.   I thought you were gonna put that away?

CLAIRE.   *(Threatening monster voice:)* What if I tortured you until you *had* to talk about it? *(She puts down squirt gun and grabs the saw from him.)*

MILLET.   Hey.

CLAIRE.   *(Grabs Millet's arm.)* What if I said I'd cut off your hand if you didn't tell me about my amnesia?!

MILLET.   *(Petrified.)* That's my puppet hand.

CLAIRE.   Tell me what happened, Millet!

MILLET.   Please!

CLAIRE.   Tell me!

MILLET.   I can't!

CLAIRE.   *(Whips off mask.)* Kidding! *(She screams with laughter. He just stares at her, frightened.)* What's the matter? *(Pause.)* I wasn't really gonna do it. I'm not like that, Millet. I don't have it in me.

MILLET.   *(Beat.)* Yes you do.

CLAIRE.   *(Pause.)* What's that supposed to mean?

MILLET.   Nothing. I promised I wouldn't — *(Puppet interrupts.)* Your husband threw the Empire State Building at your forehead.

CLAIRE.   *(Beat.)* What'd he say?

MILLET.   *(Puppet.)* It was a souvenir paperweight! *(Normal.)* Binky —

CLAIRE. *(Touches the scar on her forehead.)* Is that what this is?

MILLET. *(Puppet.)* Another time he got mad because you said his shirt was a girly shirt — *(Normal.)* You know we're not — *(Puppet.)* As a joke you said it, but he got mad! *(Normal.)* I promised! *(Puppet.)* And he threw you across the floor and poured a bowl of cereal on you and slammed your head against the oven door and you were unconscious for three hours! *(Normal.)* Stop it, Binky! *(Rips puppet off his hand.)* There. Sorry. Please don't tell him Binky said anything. He'll be so mad.

CLAIRE. Is that why my brother took me away? Because Richard Fiffle beat me up?

MILLET. I don't know! I don't know anything! *(Again, we hear the echoey dog barking, louder this time. Claire taps her head.)*

CLAIRE. Goddamnit! You don't hear barking?!

MILLET. I hate basements! *(Limping Man enters from upstairs.)*

LIMPING MAN. Hey, kidth. Everyone playing nithe?

CLAIRE. Why didn't you tell me Richard Fiffle poured cereal on me?

LIMPING MAN. Oh. Millet mentioned that?

MILLET. It was the puppet.

LIMPING MAN. Thingth can get tho complicated, Claire. And I have tho much to do today.

CLAIRE. Still …

LIMPING MAN. I can't exthplain everything to you and do everything elth, and then have you go to thleep and do it all over again tomorrow. I'm prethed for time.

CLAIRE. But he said you had a plan and —

LIMPING MAN. Forget everything Millet thed. Leth juth have a *nithe* day. Okay?

CLAIRE. But my head's all jumbled and I'm hearing barking and music and —

LIMPING MAN. You're thafe, Claire. You don't need to get all worked up about who'th who or whath what. Your brother hath taken you away from the bad man. Thath all you need to know. I'm gonna take care of you. From now on, it'll be nothing but eathy chairth and warm baked goodth. Okay?

CLAIRE. Okay. *(Smiles.)* Thank you, Zack.

LIMPING MAN. Sure. *(She kisses him on the cheek, but he turns his head, planting a kiss on her lips. It lands a little too firmly and lasts a little too long.)*

CLAIRE.   *(Pause.)* Is our family always so friendly?

LIMPING MAN.   Go have thum breakfatht. Your mom'th waiting for you. *Our* mom, I mean. *Our* mom.

CLAIRE.   *(Uneasily.)* Uhh ... okay. *(Exits.)*

MILLET.   She had a monster mask and a weird voice and you know I don't like basements. And she said she was gonna cut off my hand and —

LIMPING MAN.   *(Picks up hacksaw.)* Thtop thpeaking, Millet. I don't wanna hear you thpeak right now. *(Saws his cuff.)*

MILLET.   You shouldn't have left me alone for so long.

LIMPING MAN.   Didn't I thay don't thpeak?

MILLET.   Yeah.

LIMPING MAN.   All right then.

MILLET.   *(Side of the mouth, as puppet.)* Can I speak?

LIMPING MAN.   No. Leth jutht get thith done. *(Lights fade on Limping Man sawing cuff. Sounds of cars transition us into —)*

SCENE 6

Lights up on Richard's car. Kenny has the gun pointed at Heidi, who's seated between him and Richard in the front seat. Heidi is nervous but tries to look calm.

RICHARD.   Now remember, Kenny, once we get there, don't let your mom know we were worried. We can't upset her. Everything's good. Smile a lot when you see her.

KENNY.   If she's there, you mean.

RICHARD.   Oh she'll be there. She *has* to be there.

HEIDI.   We just crossed the state line, in case you're keeping track of the felonies you're racking up.

RICHARD.   See, this is no good. I've kidnapped a lady cop.

HEIDI.   My name's Heidi.

RICHARD.   I've kidnapped Heidi. You see why I need your mother? This is the old me. You're in a car with the old me. Can you tell?

KENNY.   I don't even know what the hell you're talking about.

RICHARD.   I try to be a good man. I get a good job at the hospital. Get a good family. And then one morning it's all gone. I'm back where I started, smokin' reefer, kidnappin' cops, crossin' state lines. It just shows ya that stability is a fragile figurine. *(Beat.)* Maybe Polly Harkness was right. I'm just a know-nothin' druggie and that's all I'll ever be.

KENNY.   Who's Polly Harkness?

RICHARD.   No one! And never mention her name again! *(Turns to Heidi suddenly.)* I love my wife so much. You understand, don't you? You ever been married?

HEIDI.   Three times.

RICHARD.   Wow. Didn't work out, huh? Husbands were no good?

HEIDI.   *(Ignores his question.)* You can still turn around, you know.

RICHARD.   Some women are just *drawn* to bad apples. Was that you?

HEIDI.   Did I mention there was a camera mounted on my dashboard?

RICHARD.   I didn't see any camera.

HEIDI.   It's very small. Records all my pull-overs. Picks up license plates real clear.

RICHARD.   Quit trying to scare me!

HEIDI.   *(Trying to sound tough.)* Well, you *should* be scared because you're in for it, buster!

RICHARD.   Buster? You people actually use that word?

HEIDI.   Yes, we use many words. It's hot in here. Can you roll down a window? Are you hot? I'm getting very hot.

RICHARD.   You seem awful nervous for a cop.

HEIDI.   Yeah well, I've got a gun in my face.

RICHARD.   We won't use it, so long as you don't try anything. I just wanna find my wife and clear my name.

HEIDI.   I said I'd forget about it if you let me go.

KENNY.   Pull over, butt-munch. She said she'd forget about it.

RICHARD. That's just a cop-trick, Kenny. They are wily, wily creatures.

HEIDI. I bet your wife's at home. I bet someone found her and brought her home.

RICHARD. On the outside Heidi seems to make sense, but underneath, she's crazy. Crazy like a fox.

KENNY. It's like you're underwater to me. Blah-blah-bloopity-bloop.

RICHARD. *(To Heidi.)* Aren't they cute at this age?

KENNY. Don't patronize me, douche bag.

RICHARD. Kenny and I have some issues to work out. Can you tell?

HEIDI. Sir, I'm losing my patience.

RICHARD. Kenny, you're the navigator. Read me the road signs.

KENNY. I'm dyslexic, moron.

HEIDI. My husbands were not bad apples. *(Kenny lights up another joint.)*

RICHARD. Kenny, don't you light up in here.

HEIDI. They were troubled, but that certainly wasn't something I was drawn to.

RICHARD. You are not gonna be all glassy-eyed when we meet your mother.

KENNY. Bite me.

RICHARD. I try to be fatherly to this kid —

HEIDI. Open the window! I'm hot and claustrophobic!

RICHARD. We need to have an intervention here.

HEIDI. I'm starting to feel like the car is shrinking.

RICHARD. I'm intervening! *(Grabs joint and throws it out the window.)*

KENNY. Hey! *(Heidi is hyperventilating.)*

RICHARD. I love you, Kenny. Heidi and I are here for you. We love you and support you.

KENNY. You make me wanna puke!

RICHARD. That's it, Kenny! I am so sick of your pissy wise-ass comments! You can go fuck yourself you miserable little prick! *(Kenny is visibly stung.)* There! How do *you* like it?

HEIDI. Jesus, I'm sweatin' like a Mexican whore!

RICHARD. *(Offended.)* Hey, watch it! My mother's half-Mexican.

HEIDI. I gotta unbutton my shirt.

RICHARD. That uniform looks too big for you. Didn't they have one your size?

HEIDI. I wear my clothes baggy.

RICHARD. Well it's not flattering. You should wear something that fits.

HEIDI. I'll give you something that fits when I shove my billy club up your ass and slap you around like a piñata!

RICHARD. You see, Kenny? The cop shows her true colors. The mask has slipped!

HEIDI. You're pissing me off and I'm claustrophobic and I don't wanna go to the country! Turn this fucking car around! *(Kenny has put the gun in his mouth.)*

KENNY. I'm gonna kill myself!

RICHARD. You think that's funny?!

HEIDI. Don't drool on my piece, nimrod!

RICHARD. What has your mother said about playing with guns?

KENNY. *(Takes gun out.)* Doesn't anyone *care?!*

RICHARD. Of course we care. *(Suddenly distracted.)* Oh look, a Denny's! I love that place.

HEIDI. *(Also pleased.)* Oooo. *(He swerves and screeches as he makes the exit. Lights out on them. The echoey carnival music transitions us into —)*

SCENE 7

Lights up on Gertie's kitchen. Gertie is buzzing around, searching for something. Claire sits at the table doing a search-a-word puzzle.

CLAIRE.   That puppet was saying the craziest things about me. Is he a trustworthy source of information?

GERTIE.   Trush noon by me, Clay.

CLAIRE.   Okay. *(Returns to search-a-word.)* Oh, I just found "banana." *(Circles it.)* What are you looking for?

GERTIE.   Dusha riddle dimsum da my hempoo. *(Rushes off to another part of the house.)*

CLAIRE.   You need any help?

GERTIE.   *(Off.)* I doan tink-toe! *(We hear one echoey bark. Claire looks up. It suddenly comes to her.)*

CLAIRE.   Nancy! Oh, I just got the bark! Mr. Cuthart's old retriever. Thank god. It was on the tip of my brain all morning. I just remembered something, Mama!

GERTIE.   *(Off.)* Dash ny!

CLAIRE.   *(Back to puzzle book.)* Oh, and here's "cantaloupe"! I'm on a roll! *(Claire circles word. Gertie enters, still searching.)* You remember that dog? Skinny old thing Mr. Cuthart kept tied up in the front lawn all day? Daddy always said he was gonna report him. Remember she just sat in the sun, biting at her scabs? Cuthart didn't even give her any water.

GERTIE.   Who do teching bat?

CLAIRE.   Nancy. So I'd sneak down the road with my squirt gun, and spritz water into her mouth and she'd bark.

GERTIE.   Uh-huh. I bee rye bag. *(Rushes off to another part of the house.)*

CLAIRE.   And one day, when Cuthart was downtown, I untied her to let her run around a little. But she darted straight into the road, just as Daddy's pickup was coming around the curve, and he

34

didn't see her, so he plowed into her. *(Calls off.)* Do you remember Daddy and I came through the back door, Mama? And Nancy was hanging out of his arms like a set of broken-up bagpipes. And he spread her out on the kitchen floor and she was breathing real hard. And the pain was humming off of her like I could hear it. And she just let the pain take her over. And that's all she was. This *pained* thing. *(Gertie enters with a cookie tin. Claire's story has brought her back into the room.)* And Daddy was bent over her, talking to her real quiet. And all of sudden Nancy stood up, like it was a new day, and she started running around the kitchen like she wasn't half-dead, barking and clicking her nails against the floor tiles. And we were all shocked because Nancy was like a puppy all of a sudden, not that bony heap on the floor. She was this fireball for about three minutes, until she got tired again, and curled up beside the sink and went to sleep and died like it meant nothing. You remember how all that happened in here? It's funny how almost everything else is gone to me, and that sad old dog just came into my head.

GERTIE. *(Hands her tin.)* Clay …

CLAIRE. Cookies? You're tearin' this place apart for cookies?

GERTIE. Pen-o, Clay. Toe-phoes. *(Gertie looks to the basement, worried. Claire opens the tin and pulls out some old photos.)*

CLAIRE. Ooo, pictures. *(Picks up photo.)* Is this me? This little girl is me, isn't it? Oh what a cutie I was.

GERTIE. Cutie Clay.

CLAIRE. *(Another photo.)* That's you and … Daddy?

GERTIE. *(Nods.)* Mm-hmm.

CLAIRE. In front of the tree that Zack climbed. Happy-happy-people. *(Another photo.)* Oh, what … what's this? It's all weird.

GERTIE. Za.

CLAIRE. Zack?

GERTIE. Ada fay. Ih da fuhnus. Da meers.

CLAIRE. Meers?

GERTIE. Ih da fuhnus. Fuddy meers. *(Holds up reflective tin cover.)* Meers.

CLAIRE. Mirrors?

GERTIE. Ih Piehmoe.

CLAIRE. Piermont? The Piermont Fair?

35

GERTIE.   Da Piehmoe Fay!

CLAIRE.   We went every spring.

GERTIE.   An da Za in da fuddy meers.

CLAIRE.   The fun-house mirrors.

GERTIE.   Yada tooda pitue oh Za ih da fuddy meers.

CLAIRE.   This is Zack? He looks all warped and twisted-up. This isn't Zack.

GERTIE.   Edadly!

CLAIRE.   I don't understand.

GERTIE.   Da ih Za, Clay. He feh oh da tee.

CLAIRE.   In the fun house, but this isn't —

GERTIE.   You doe mem ohta tins dah happy. *(The echoey carnival music pipes in. Claire taps her head with the palm of her hand.)*

CLAIRE.   Oops. Here we go again. Music time.

GERTIE.   Clay?

CLAIRE.   It'll pass in a second. Although … *(Struggles with a memory.)* I'm seeing a frying pan. Should that ring any bells?

GERTIE.   Yesh! Da fyin pay! *(We hear the men approaching.)*

LIMPING MAN.   *(Off.)* Letth load theethe thleeping bagth into the back of the car.

MILLET.   *(Off, as puppet.)* I bet they're musty and crawling with bugs!

GERTIE.   Dogdambit! *(Gertie gathers up photos and pushes tin aside. The music stops.)*

CLAIRE.   There. It's gone again. *(Millet and Limping Man enter, cuffless.)*

LIMPING MAN.   You were good, right Gertie? Played by the roolth? Like we thaid?

GERTIE.   Cursive. Ida nevoo crotch you.

LIMPING MAN.   Good. You've been a firth-clath hothteth. But our party ith moving on.

MILLET.   *(Puppet.)* No more manacles, see?

CLAIRE.   Where you going, Zack?

LIMPING MAN.   Jutht for a drive. Grab your thtuff. Letth go!

MILLET.   I didn't know she was coming with us.

CLAIRE.   I wanna stay with Mama.

LIMPING MAN.   Claire, we need to get you thomewhere thafe.

You don't think that huthband of yourth ithn't gonna figure thith out? You don't think he'th gonna make hith way to Gertie'th houthe?

CLAIRE. I don't really know him that well.

LIMPING MAN. Egthactly. Thath why you need to rely on me. He'll find you. Won't he, Gertie? Tell Claire here that she needth to leave with me and Millet.

MILLET. That wasn't the plan. I thought you just wanted to talk to her.

LIMPING MAN. Go warm up the car.

MILLET. *(As puppet.)* He's not warming up nothing, gimpy!

LIMPING MAN. Binky —

CLAIRE. I don't want to go for a drive.

MILLET. *(As puppet.)* She doesn't wanna go for a drive.

LIMPING MAN. Millet —

MILLET. Binky —

GERTIE. Clay —

LIMPING MAN. Gertie, explain to her how she hath to go with uth.

GERTIE. Noda Za, Clay. Ee feh oh da tee.

LIMPING MAN. Gertie'th had a thtroke. She geth all muddled thometimth. Right, Gertie?

GERTIE. *(To Limping Man.)* Yuca keelush, Fee, buhda woe cha-cha nuddy!

LIMPING MAN. Thtroke victimth are eathily upthet. She'th like thith all the time.

MILLET. *(As puppet.)* Lies, Millet! All lies!

LIMPING MAN. *(To Millet.)* Get the mapth out of the glove compartment —

MILLET. That wasn't the plan!

LIMPING MAN. And review the route. *(Gertie has opened tin and pulled out old newspaper article.)*

GERTIE. *(Pushing article at Claire.)* Ree, Clay! Ree!

MILLET. *(Puppet to Limping Man.)* You're not in charge of him!

CLAIRE. *(Looking at article.)* What is this?

MILLET. *(Puppet to Limping Man.)* You're not his mother!

GERTIE. Ih tess wha happy!

LIMPING MAN. What'd you give her, Gertie?!

37

CLAIRE. It's Zack's obituary.

LIMPING MAN. She'th crazy, Claire. Ever thince the thtroke.

CLAIRE. It says Zack died when he was eight. *(Limping Man grabs obituary from Claire.)*

MILLET. We had *meetings* about the plan.

GERTIE. He feh oh da tee!

CLAIRE. He fell out of the tree!

MILLET. And now everything changes all of a sudden.

LIMPING MAN. *(To Millet.)* Get in the fucking car!

CLAIRE. He climbed too high and fell.

LIMPING MAN. Thath a different boy, Claire!

CLAIRE. Zack died. *(Kenny, Heidi and Richard, holding up bacon, appear in the window.)*

RICHARD. Somebody lose some bacon? *(Everyone screams.)* What the devil's going on here?

CLAIRE. *(To Richard.)* Stay away! They told me everything!

RICHARD. I'm coming around the front! *(Richard, Kenny and Heidi exit window.)*

CLAIRE. Oh no, he's coming around the front! *(Gertie grabs kitchen knife and raises it.)*

LIMPING MAN. Claire, quick, out the window!

GERTIE. Egg dis! *(Gertie stabs Limping Man in the back. He screams and falls to the ground in pain.)*

MILLET. What's happening?!

LIMPING MAN. The old crone thtabbed me!

MILLET. Aw geez!

LIMPING MAN. Don't you leave me, Millet!

MILLET. This is bad. This is very bad. *(Gertie rushes to phone and dials 911.)*

CLAIRE. Mama, I gotta hide from Richard Fiffle!

MILLET. This is what happens when we change the plan.

GERTIE. *(Into phone.)* Isis Geht Maso! *Fee cape!* I dabbed him inda bag! *(Millet is about to run out when Richard runs in, followed by Kenny, who leads Heidi in at gunpoint.)*

MILLET. It's the cops! *(Tries to hide.)*

KENNY. What the hell?!

RICHARD. *(To Heidi.)* Look! What did I tell you? Claire!

CLAIRE. *(To Richard.)* Stay away from me!

GERTIE. *(Into phone.)* Ona four ohda clickin! *(Sees Heidi.)* Oh, dear heah.

LIMPING MAN. Millet, call a doctor!

MILLET. Okay, call a doctor.

KENNY. Are you okay, Mom?

CLAIRE. Gertie stabbed the deformed man!

MILLET. *(To Gertie.)* Gimme the phone!

GERTIE. No! Iss my-pho! Fug-dew!

RICHARD. Claire —

CLAIRE. *(Runs away.)* Help!

RICHARD. Would someone tell her I'm the nice guy?!

HEIDI. *(Going to Limping Man.)* Who did this to you?

LIMPING MAN. *(Points to Gertie.)* She did! She did it!

HEIDI. *(To Kenny.)* All right, gimme my gun.

KENNY. No way, that's my grandmother. *(In the confusion, Heidi tries to wrestle the gun from Kenny's hand. They struggle while Limping Man writhes on the ground. Millet tries to get phone from Gertie. Richard pursues Claire.)*

RICHARD. But Claire, we've been looking for you.

CLAIRE. I heard about the paperweight!

HEIDI. *(Struggling with Kenny.)* Let go of the gun, pot-head!

LIMPING MAN. *(Referring to Gertie.)* Knock her out, Millet!

MILLET. *(As puppet, struggling with Gertie.)* Don't tell him what to do!

KENNY. You're gonna shoot the wrong people!

GERTIE. Ah! My pho!

MILLET. *(As puppet.)* My-pho! My-pho!

RICHARD. You were safe with me, Claire.

CLAIRE. Get him away!

LIMPING MAN. You thcrewed me, Gertie! You shouldn't have done that! *(Gertie snatches the puppet and raises the knife.)*

GERTIE. Dab da fuddin puppa! *(Stabs the puppet repeatedly.)*

MILLET. Ah! Hinky Binky! *(As puppet.)* Help! She's killing me! *(All overlapping.)*

HEIDI.	LIMPING MAN.
It's *my* gun! You drugged-out little twirp!	I'm bleeding to death! Stupid old lady! Look what you did!

MILLET.
She's killing me! Oh, the pain is unbearable!

KENNY.
Let go of it! You don't know who anybody is!

RICHARD.
It's okay, Claire. Don't believe anything this man has told you.

GERTIE.
Kee da puppa! Doopy fuddin puppa! Die! Die!

(A cacophony of noise from all of them. Gertie stabbing Hinky Binky. Kenny wrestling with Heidi. Richard pursuing Claire. Millet screaming as the puppet. Limping Man in agony. Then Claire lets out a long wail.)

CLAIRE. Stoooooooooooooooooooopppppp iiiiiiiiiiiiiiit! *(The gun goes off. Blackout.)*

END OF ACT ONE

ACT TWO

SCENE 1

In darkness we hear the gunshot. Lights up on Gertie's kitchen, where we left off. Claire seems to be a little out of it. Kenny has been shot in the arm.

KENNY.   Aawwwww, god. *(Holds his arm in pain.)*

RICHARD.   Are you okay, Kenny?

KENNY.   I've been shot!

LIMPING MAN.   I've been thtabbed!

MILLET.   My Binky got cut!

GERTIE.   An noon onion stammy!

HEIDI.   *(Stands with gun.)* Anyone moves, I'll shoot you a new asshole!

RICHARD.   *(To Heidi.)* Now you see why I was in a hurry? Check my wife. She has amnesia.

HEIDI.   Don't tell me what to do!

GERTIE.   *(Points frantically at Limping Man.)* Ish axel is genderlish!

HEIDI.   *What?!*

GERTIE.   Ee hersh poopoos!

RICHARD.   She's absolutely right.

HEIDI.   Millet —

MILLET.   Yes?

HEIDI.   Get the knife.

MILLET.   But Hinky Binky got hurt and —

HEIDI.   Just get the knife. *(Everyone's confused. Millet takes knife from Gertie.)*

GERTIE.   I doan onion stammish.

MILLET.   Here's the knife.

41

HEIDI. Good. Now if anyone moves, stab them in the head. *(Indicates Richard.)* And watch this bozo. He knows how to disarm people. *(Goes to Limping Man.)* How you doing, baby? Got stabbed, huh?

LIMPING MAN. You were thuppothed to watch them. You were thuppothed to detain them and make sure they didn't get up here.

HEIDI. Well, it didn't go as planned.

KENNY. *(Realizing.)* Oh, man …

RICHARD. Do you all know each other?

LIMPING MAN. Did you get the pathportth?

HEIDI. Yeah, Twitchy hooked me up with a guy in Bingham.

CLAIRE. Would someone tell me what's going on? *(Beat.)* Would someone tell me one bit of truthful information … please? *(Silence. They all look around at each other. After a couple beats, Gertie finally steps forward to clear things up.)*

GERTIE. Ida gnome mower, Clay. Evatin row when Za feh oda tee. Da die. Oomay Fee an bah tin happy. Deh oo fie bah an deh figit. An I hada toke, so king talk bah. Fee heah an evatin bah gin. Evatin bah gin, Clay.

CLAIRE. *(Beat.)* What the fuck are you talking about?!!!

RICHARD. Claire …

CLAIRE. *(Banging palms against her head.)* I'm sorry. I'm not myself today.

RICHARD. Don't whack your head, honey.

HEIDI. *(Comforting Limping Man.)* Aww, look at Mr. Bloody.

KENNY. Oh, I'm sorry, did I mention I've been shot? Well I *was!*

LIMPING MAN. Claire wath a nurth. She can help uth.

CLAIRE. *(Stops banging head.)* What?

HEIDI. Millet, take the husband and the old lady to the basement.

MILLET. But my freebasing mom used to lock me in the basement!

CLAIRE. I was a nurse?

MILLET. We have to go back to the plan!

LIMPING MAN. All right, we'll go back to the plan!

CLAIRE. Did I wear nurse's shoes?

KENNY. I'll tell you what happened, Mom.

RICHARD and LIMPING MAN. Kenny, no! *(Richard and Limping Man look at each other.)*

RICHARD. Remember what the doctors said, Kenny. There were strict instructions.

LIMPING MAN. Better lithen to your dad. *(Kenny turns his attention to his wound.)*

HEIDI. Get them out of here, Millet.

MILLET. *(To Richard and Gertie.)* I have to lock ya in the basement.

RICHARD. *(To Claire.)* Nothing to worry about, Claire. Everything's gonna be jim-dandy!

MILLET. Keep moving! *(Leads Gertie and Richard to the basement.)*

KENNY. Hello! Bullet wound on the child! Am I *invisible*?!

HEIDI. You were *grazed*.

KENNY. I'm still *bleeding*, bitch.

HEIDI. *(To Claire.)* You're raising a misogynist. You're a terrible mother.

CLAIRE. I am? Oh dear. I thought I might be.

LIMPING MAN. Look at all the carnage. Remindth me of when I wath in Nam.

KENNY. You were never in Nam.

CLAIRE. Okay, maybe we need supplies. Nurse's supplies. Let's see, what do I need? *(Beat.)* I guess I don't know what we need.

HEIDI. She's useless.

KENNY. She has amnesia, dumb-ass.

HEIDI. *(Hands gun to Limping Man.)* Take the gun. I'm gonna check the medicine cabinet. If they try anything, shoot them in the head. *(Exits.)*

CLAIRE. She seems to have a bit of a chip on her shoulder. *(Turns to Kenny.)* Hey, what kind of nurse was I anyway?

KENNY. A school nurse.

CLAIRE. Oh, I bet my uniform was very starched.

LIMPING MAN. *(Grabs nearby towel.)* Take thith, Kenny. Hold it tight to thtop thome of the bleeding.

KENNY. Fuck you.

LIMPING MAN. You're an angry little man. Thath a terrible

43

thing to be. *(Claire takes towel and brings it to Kenny's arm.)*
CLAIRE.   Yes, apply pressure, stop the bleeding. This is familiar.
All those kids running in from the playground with scrapes and
cuts and cigarette burns and souvenir paperweights sticking out of
their foreheads. *(Beat.)* Is that right? That doesn't seem right to me.
LIMPING MAN.   Hey, Claire?
CLAIRE.   Yeah, Zack?
KENNY.   His name is Philip.
CLAIRE.   Right. He's *Philip* pretending to be Zack who fell out
of the tree. Sorry. It's so hard to keep it all straight.
LIMPING MAN.   Look at my back. Can you thtitch
it up?
CLAIRE.   *(Examines his back.)* Oh sure. I've seen much worse
than that. God knows I don't know *where*. *(Moves to Kenny.)* No
stitches for you, Kenny. Just a nice clean bandage. *(Pause as she
looks at him.)* I wasn't really a bad mother, was I? What the lady
just said, is it true?
KENNY.   No. She doesn't know you. You were a good mother.
CLAIRE.   Oh good. *(Remembers.)* Six pounds, fourteen ounces.
(Beat.) That's how much you weighed at birth.
KENNY.   *(Wants to tell her.)* Mom ...
CLAIRE.   Yes?
KENNY.   *(Looks over at Limping Man.)* Never mind. *(Lights out
on them. The echoey dog barking transitions us into —)*

SCENE 2

Lights up in the basement. Millet stands guard over Richard and Gertie.

MILLET.   Nobody better try anything 'cause I've been tricked too many times today.

GERTIE.   Dash biggo yoo-zo doopy.

MILLET.   Don't talk jibberish. I'm sure you just said something very mean about me. *(As puppet.)* So ... much ... pain ... *(Normal.)* And look what you did to Hinky Binky. *(Puppet.)* Everything's going dark. *(Normal.)* Hang in there, Bink. *(Puppet.)* Millet, is that you? *(Normal.)* I'm here. Be brave, little puppet.

RICHARD.   Damn. You're crazy.

MILLET.   You got a sewing kit in this dungeon?

GERTIE.   Yah. Maybe ova nose bachus.

MILLET.   Well, go get it. I gotta fix my friend.

GERTIE.   Uh ... oday. Aybee ride bag. *(Gertie goes off into other part of the basement.)*

MILLET.   I'm watching you, old lady, so don't get funny.

GERTIE.   *(Off.)* Nuddin fuddy heah.

RICHARD.   Look, I don't know what you people have in mind, but it's not worth wrecking your life. Believe me, I know.

MILLET.   I'm not talking to you. Talk gets me in trouble. My lip is zipped, Sporto.

RICHARD.   I know where your head is right now. You're probably strung out, doin' whatever you can to scrounge up the next fix.

MILLET.   What?

RICHARD.   Sure, I look like an upright guy, nice family, good job at the hospital, but I've been right where you're standing, buddy-boy.

MILLET.   *(Calls off.)* Gertie, my Binky is dying!

GERTIE.   *(Off.)* Ahm dill loodin!

RICHARD. She said she's still looking.

MILLET. I know what she said.

GERTIE. *(Crosses with a photo album.)* I tink iss up in da clickin. *(Exits upstairs.)*

MILLET. Hey! She's a slippery one, isn't she?

RICHARD. You gotta open your eyes, my friend. You are mixed up with a *very* bad crowd.

MILLET. *(Weak puppet.)* I can't feel my toes.

RICHARD. I was in deep, just like you. And *I* got out.

MILLET. *(Weak puppet.)* Are you a doctor?

RICHARD. *(Beat.)* No. I work at the hospital but I'm just a technician. I run the MRIs. That's how I met Claire.

MILLET. *(Weak puppet.)* So, you can't help me ... MRI guy?

RICHARD. I'm sorry, puppet. I can't.

MILLET. *(Normal.)* We'll stitch you up in no time, Binky.

RICHARD. This is crazy — this is — this is — *(Loses it.)* There is a woman upstairs with a *medical* condition! She is probably very disoriented and frightened and in physical danger and if that guy — !!!

MILLET. Stop yelling at me! Why are you yelling at me?!

RICHARD. I'm sorry. I just ... I should never have taken that shower.

GERTIE. *(Off.)* I gut da doe-in-tit.

RICHARD. Someday, if you're very lucky, you're gonna get everything you ever wanted in life. And when someone tries to take it away, then you'll understand why I was yelling. *(Gertie comes back carrying a sewing kit and a photo album.)*

GERTIE. Heah da doe-in-tit. *(Hands sewing kit to Millet.)*

MILLET. I'm gonna stay over here and sew up Binky. Nobody come near me. I've got a knife.

RICHARD. You're not gonna use it.

MILLET. Oh shut up.

GERTIE. Loo ah dese toe-phos, Record. *(She brings album to Richard. They flip through it.)*

RICHARD. I'm not really in the mood to look at photos, Gert.

GERTIE. Loo ah dis one dough. Is da weddin dah.

RICHARD. Gosh, look at that. Claire in a wedding dress. So young. *(Spots another photo.)* And is that Phil doing the chicken dance?

GERTIE. Sumna-bitch.

RICHARD. Weird. He looks normal. Nice ears. Both sides working.

GERTIE. Mean sumnabitch.

RICHARD. *(Another photo.)* And there's you with the bouquet. You look mad.

GERTIE. I coo tah den. Bach den evabiddy onion stammy. I wizz-eye hat ... *(Tries very hard to say this.)* Iiii wiissh ... I had ... sehd sssummttiiinnn weeeehnn ... I c-could.

RICHARD. *(Pause.)* You know what I wish? I wish I never did drugs, or robbed houses, or resisted arrest, but I did all those things. And the best I can do is make up for it.

MILLET. I stole some toilet paper from the janitor's closet once. I felt terrible about that, but I was all out at home.

RICHARD. *(New photo.)* That's a nice photo of you, Gert. Digging out in the garden ... Digging with your *shovel*.

GERTIE. Digga widda shova.

MILLET. *(Still sewing.)* Digga widda shova.

GERTIE. Aybee rye bag. *(Runs off into other part of basement.)*

MILLET. Come back here! I'm guarding you!

GERTIE. *(Off.)* Toe-phoes! Thall! Toe-phoes!

MILLET. I'm a terrible guard.

RICHARD. What's your name anyway?

MILLET. Millet. *(Reconsiders suddenly.)* I mean Hector.

RICHARD. Don't you wanna change, Millet?

MILLET. My name is Hector I said!

RICHARD. Isn't there something you've always wanted to do? Be a teacher? A lawyer?

MILLET. *(Puppet.)* Zookeeper. He always wanted to be a zookeeper. *(Normal. Happy to see the puppet has recovered.)* Binky!

RICHARD. Well there you go. You can do that. It's not too late to be a zookeeper. And the first step is helping us, because you know it's right.

MILLET. Phil is here to make up with her. I *am* doing right.

RICHARD. You don't believe that. You know he's lied to you like he's lied to everyone.

MILLET. I'm not listening! *(Gertie, rummaging, knocks something over.)*

GERTIE. *(Off.)* Dem pick gog shit! Fuddin shit!

RICHARD. This hostage stuff isn't the life you want. Kidnapping an innocent woman, lying to her, getting her family upset ...

MILLET. *(Puppet adds to list.)* Bringing her to Canada.

RICHARD. Canada?

MILLET. Binky!

RICHARD. He's bringing Claire to Canada?

MILLET. *(To Richard.)* Don't talk to us! I hate this basement! It's like truth serum!

RICHARD. Claire doesn't wanna go to Canada, and you know that. You can end it here. You just stop and say, "I've had enough. Today I'm a good person." That's what I did. And it worked.

MILLET. How?

RICHARD. I'll tell you how. Polly Harkness.

MILLET. Gertie?!

GERTIE. *(Off.)* I'm loodin!

RICHARD. I loved that woman more than life. She worked at the hardware store. And I wanted to marry her, but I didn't have any money to get a ring, so I got stoned and decided to find a lady with the same size fingers, and rob her. Take *her* wedding ring.

MILLET. *(Something bothers him.)* You were gonna steal somebody's ring?

RICHARD. I was a bad man. Now you see how we're the same?

GERTIE. *(Off.)* I ding I fow da bach, Record!

RICHARD. I searched all day and finally spotted a lady with the same size and build coming out of a school, getting into her car. She never saw me. I knocked her over the head with a rock and she was out. And I took her ring.

MILLET. *(Still trying to figure it out.)* With a nice diamond in the middle, and two rubies on the side?

RICHARD. Right. I offered it to Polly on my knees, and she said no. Because there was blood on it. And she'd never marry a know-nothin' druggie. So I decided to change, mostly to spite her. I went back to school and learned how to run the MRI machines, and that's how I met Claire. And guess who's wearing that ring right now?

GERTIE. *(Off.)* Damma fuddin shova!

RICHARD. Now do you see what you can accomplish?

MILLET. I knew that ring looked familiar. I'm so stupid!

RICHARD. You okay, Gertie?!

MILLET. You can't hurt people like that and have someone else take the blame!

GERTIE. *(Off.)* I guddit!

MILLET. *(Stalking Richard.)* You can't hurt people like that.

RICHARD. I don't anymore. That's my point.

MILLET. You should never hurt people. Never. *(Millet chases Richard into the darkness of the basement offstage. From a different part of the basement, Gertie comes running out of the darkness with a raised shovel. She runs after an oblivious Millet. Offstage we hear the metallic thwack of a shovel hitting his head. Lights out. A strange jumbled overlapping of carnival music, dog barking, the '70s easy-listening song and radio scanning transitions us into —)*

SCENE 3

Lights up in the kitchen. Claire is bandaging Kenny's arm. Limping Man tries to thread a needle. Heidi is pacing.

HEIDI. Jesus! This is taking too long. *(To Claire.)* Stitch up his back.

CLAIRE. *(Still with Kenny.)* Almost done.

HEIDI. You said we'd be in and out. You said "a few words."

LIMPING MAN. And you thaid you'd watch the huthband!

HEIDI. This is screwy. Some big apology to someone who isn't even gonna remember it.

LIMPING MAN. I'll remember it.

CLAIRE. Ooo, there's an apology coming?

HEIDI. We don't have a lot of time, Phil.

CLAIRE. Excuse me, did you help him break out of jail?

HEIDI. Yes I did. We're in love.

CLAIRE. Gosh, a convict and a lady cop.

HEIDI. I'm not really a lady cop. I just stole the uniform from the laundry truck.

LIMPING MAN.   What are you doing?

HEIDI.   It's not like she's gonna remember. *(To Claire.)* I'm really a kitchen worker. I prepare the prison meals.

KENNY.   You're a lunch lady?

HEIDI.   I do dinners too!

CLAIRE.   And you met in the kitchen?

HEIDI.   Yeah. Phil was on dish duty. He caught my eye while scraping plates.

CLAIRE.   How sweet. And now you're on the lam. You must really love each other.

HEIDI.   I just said we did.

CLAIRE.   Did you? Oh, I must've forgot. Did Philip say it too? Because I don't remember him mentioning it.

LIMPING MAN.   You almotht done there, Claire?

HEIDI.   Hey, he loves me, okay? We're going to Canada together. Tell her how we're going to Canada.

LIMPING MAN.   We're going to Canada.

HEIDI.   I'm gonna tell you something, lady. I went out on a limb for this man. I laced the guards' pulled-pork sandwiches. Have you ever done anything like that for him?

CLAIRE.   I don't know.

HEIDI.   I love him, you understand? And he loves me. Don't you, Phil? *(Pause.)* Phil?

CLAIRE.   He's deaf in that ear. Maybe he didn't hear you.

HEIDI.   Don't you love me, Phil?!

LIMPING MAN.   *(Pause.)* Of courth I do.

HEIDI.   *(Turns to Claire.)* See? I told you.

CLAIRE.   Can you get me some ice from the freezer? *(Heidi goes to the freezer. To Limping Man:)* You got yourself a firecracker there. *(To Kenny.)* All done.

KENNY.   Thanks.

CLAIRE.   *(To Limping Man.)* Your turn. *(Gertie enters from the basment, carrying a photo album.)*

GERTIE.   Heddo, dis geddin da doe-in-tit. *(Gertie grabs the sewing kit, leaving behind a few needles and spools of thread. She calls down into basement.)* I gut da doe-in-tit. *(Exits into basment.)*

LIMPING MAN.   *(Referring to Millet.)* He's a terrible guard. *(Heidi comes back with frozen food items. Claire cleans Phil's*

50

wound.)

HEIDI.   No ice. Just frozen food. Ground beef, Tater-Tots, a pound of bacon —
LIMPING MAN.   No bacon! Put the bacon back! You should know! What did I thay about bacon?!
HEIDI.   *(Pause.)* I'm sorry. I'll put the bacon back. *(She does. Claire holds frozen food to Philip's back. He winces.)*
CLAIRE.   It's very odd.
LIMPING MAN.   What?
CLAIRE.   This whole bacon thing.
LIMPING MAN.   I don't wanna talk about it.
CLAIRE.   Are you a vegetarian?
LIMPING MAN.   Am I what?
HEIDI.   He's just mad because I blabbed.
LIMPING MAN.   Well Jethuth, Heidi, the whole plan hinged on abtholute thecrethy!
HEIDI.   She has *amnesia!*
LIMPING MAN.   The *boy* has ears!
KENNY.   Yeah, nice ones too. Not like my dad's.
LIMPING MAN.   Kenny —
CLAIRE.   What's he talking about?
LIMPING MAN.   Nothing. Your kidth a little thlow. He thez weird thingth all the time.
KENNY.   This guy's my father.
LIMPING MAN.   Goddamnit, Kenny.
CLAIRE.   What?
KENNY.   You were married to him for nineteen years.
CLAIRE.   I thought Richard Fiffle was my husband.
KENNY.   *Second* husband.
LIMPING MAN.   I wath waiting for the right time to tell you.
HEIDI.   He's really sorry. *(To Limping Man.)* Can we go now?
CLAIRE.   Sorry for what?
KENNY.   Dad's got a short fuse, and a killer left hook.
LIMPING MAN.   Kenny, you are breaking the roolth! *(Turns to Claire.)* Look, I wath gonna tell you everything. But then they all popped up in the window and the puppet thcreamed and Gertie thtuck a knife in my back.
CLAIRE.   Why were you in jail?

KENNY.   He set our house on fire.

LIMPING MAN.   I wath provoked!

CLAIRE.   You burned our house down?

LIMPING MAN.   I yoothed to have a temper, but I'm thweeter than cuthtard now. Athk Heidi.

HEIDI.   Just put in the stitches so we can go.

LIMPING MAN.   I've had a lot of countheling.

KENNY.   Sounds like you've made great strides.

HEIDI.   Shoot him! *Shoot* him!

LIMPING MAN.   Heidi, I'm not gonna shoot my own kid. *(Beat.)* A couple yearth ago, I might've, but not anymore.

HEIDI.   Gimme that fucking needle, I'll do it myself. *(Grabs sewing supplies.)*

LIMPING MAN.   Heidi, you don't know how to —

HEIDI.   I took Home Ec! *(Gets to work on sewing his wound.)*

KENNY.   Tell her the rest!

LIMPING MAN.   Kenny, you don't know how good I was in prithon.

CLAIRE.   *(More to herself.)* Richard Fiffle didn't beat me.

LIMPING MAN.   *(Stuck by needle.)* Ow!

HEIDI.   Sorry.

CLAIRE.   Zack and I were playing. And he fell.

LIMPING MAN.   I worked hard, Claire. And rehabilitated mythelf.

HEIDI.   Hold still.

LIMPING MAN.   I did crafth. Made dioramath out of popthicle thtickth.

CLAIRE.   You lied when you took me away.

LIMPING MAN.   I read the Bible.

HEIDI.   He wrote me poems.

CLAIRE.   You wrote her poems?

LIMPING MAN.   *(To Claire.)* You were the inthpiration. *(Stuck by needle.)* Ow!

HEIDI.   No she wasn't.

LIMPING MAN.   *(In pain.)* Jethuth, Heidi.

CLAIRE.   *(Sorting it out.)* And Nancy died here.

HEIDI.   Those poems were mine, Phil. *(To Claire.)* He wrote one called "Heidi's Hairnet." *(To Phil.)* It wasn't called "*Claire's*

Hairnet."

KENNY. Tell her the rest. Before jail.

LIMPING MAN. Kenny — *(Stuck.)* Heidi!

KENNY. Do you remember my birthday, Mom?

CLAIRE. May third.

KENNY. May third. She's coming back strong. Do you remember the day I turned fifteen?

CLAIRE. No.

KENNY. It was almost two years ago, the day your brain zorched.

LIMPING MAN. Come on, she doethn't —

KENNY. You said you were gonna tell her everything.

CLAIRE. You did say that, Phil.

LIMPING MAN. Yeah but I — ow!

CLAIRE. Fifteenth birthday. Go on.

KENNY. The plan was, you were gonna take me to the Piermont Fair.

CLAIRE. That's where my dad took me and Zack.

KENNY. Exactly what you said. Sounded like fun. And Phil didn't wanna go.

LIMPING MAN. I don't like fairth.

KENNY. Which was fine by me.

LIMPING MAN. Carnieth give me the creepth.

KENNY. So that morning, we got up early. You set out the Fruity Pebbles and we were about to leave. Only he woke up and said he didn't want no Fruity Pebbles, he wanted a *hot* breakfast.

LIMPING MAN. I wathn't feeling good, Claire. I needed thomething thubthtantial in my thtomach.

KENNY. But we were about to go, so I asked him why he couldn't make his own breakfast, which I guess was out of line.

LIMPING MAN. Look, whath important ith I've changed.

KENNY. Because he leaned back, made a fist and clocked me.

LIMPING MAN. That wath the only time I hit that kid. Tell her that.

KENNY. He's right. He knocked you against the wall every day of the week, but that was the only time he hit me.

LIMPING MAN. I did not hit you every day. He exaggerayth.

HEIDI. I said don't move.

KENNY. So I'm sitting there, cartoon birdies flying around my head —

LIMPING MAN. He'th not remembering it right.

KENNY. And he starts throwing things around the kitchen.

LIMPING MAN. Nothing breakable.

KENNY. Things broke.

LIMPING MAN. Thith kid'th not right in the head, Claire.

KENNY. And he's over me screaming that fifteen is too old to go to a fair. That it must be a fairy fair.

LIMPING MAN. You won't remember thith, but I dropped him ath a baby. All the time.

KENNY. And you're just standing at the stove.

LIMPING MAN. I wath a total butterfingerth.

KENNY. Making him the eggs and bacon he asked for.

LIMPING MAN. Tho hith head ith a little off.

HEIDI. Also he's stoned.

KENNY. I remember this!

LIMPING MAN. Claire, I'm here to apologithe. I wish none of that happened. Thath why I'm here.

KENNY. Hold on, we're getting to the good part.

LIMPING MAN. Ow!

KENNY. You're frying up the bacon, nice and crisp the way he likes it, and he says —

LIMPING MAN. I'm not a unique perthon.

KENNY. And he says, "Never mind, I'm not hungry anymore."

LIMPING MAN. Many men hit people. And a lot of them learn how to thtop.

KENNY. And he goes into the bedroom and slams the door.

CLAIRE. And he falls back to sleep.

KENNY. (Beat.) That's right. Because a good tantrum always knocked him out.

CLAIRE. And I tell you to go wait in the car …

LIMPING MAN. Claire —

CLAIRE. — because we were going to Piermont.

KENNY. So I limp to the car.

CLAIRE. And I pick up the frying pan and walk into the bedroom, and he's sleeping on his side. And I drain the scalding bacon grease into his ear.

KENNY.   And I hear the scream through the bedroom door, and the storm door and the screen door and the car door. All those doors but I can still hear that scream.

CLAIRE.   And I come outside and throw the frying pan into the bushes and get in the car. And we drive to Piermont in silence. *(Pause.)* And then what happened?

KENNY.   We rode on the ferris wheel

CLAIRE.   Uh-huh.

KENNY.   And the tilt-a-whirl.

CLAIRE.   Right.

KENNY.   And we went to the fun house.

CLAIRE.   And in the fun house were the funny mirrors that made everything all warped and stretched.

KENNY.   And you said your brother Zack loved that best.

CLAIRE.   He did.

KENNY.   And you said the two of you would dance in the funny mirrors and your dad would take pictures of the twisted reflections.

CLAIRE.   I said that?

KENNY.   Yeah.

CLAIRE.   And then what happened?

KENNY.   You fainted. And when you woke up, everything was gone. You didn't remember anything. It was all gone. *(Silence.)*

LIMPING MAN.   Well whoopty-doo. There you have it, all wrapped in a big red bow. *(To Kenny.)* You done, kid?

CLAIRE.   You shouldn't be so flip.

LIMPING MAN.   But Claire, the whole point ith I'm not that perthon anymore.

HEIDI.   *(Breaks thread.)* You're done. Let's go.

LIMPING MAN.   Look, I'm thorry I thet the houthe on fire while you were at the fair. I wath mad. But now ... now I'm glad you poured that ... bacon greathe in my ear. You know why? Becauthe it burned the bad part out of me. The bad bit ith a dead bulb. Only the good parth twinkle now.

KENNY.   *(To Limping Man.)* You can leave.

LIMPING MAN.   We're gonna go to Canada. Millet hath a friend who'll hide uth. *(Beat.)* Come with uth, Claire.

HEIDI.   Phil —

LIMPING MAN.   Whath one more perthon?

HEIDI.   This wasn't the plan.

LIMPING MAN.   Planth change.

HEIDI.   You said *talk* to her, not *bring* her.

LIMPING MAN.   Claire, we can thtart over.

HEIDI.   You motherfucker.

LIMPING MAN.   Heidi, you gotta underthtand.

HEIDI.   Suck my ass, Phil.

LIMPING MAN.   Juth go get Millet. We'll all talk about it.

HEIDI.   Yeah, I'll go get Millet, and then he and I will leave here without you.

LIMPING MAN.   Heidi — *(Reaches out to her.)*

HEIDI.   Don't touch me! I am not her! I'll kick the shit of you, you deformed monkey! *(Calls off.)* Millet?! *(Exits into basement.)*

LIMPING MAN.   *(Beat.)* Thath okay. We can take my car. *(Claire doesn't move.)* Come on, Claire. It wathn't all like he thaid. *(To Kenny.)* Tell her about the Monopoly gaymth. And the thurch-a-wordth. *(To Claire.)* We would do thurch-a-word puthelth together. You and me, on the couch. And I'd braid your hair. Remember how I'd braid your hair? *(No response.)* I love you, Claire. We've shared a life. For better or worth, it wath ourth. And I love you. Now leth go. *(Kenny makes a mad scramble for the gun. Limping Man is confused. Kenny suddenly has the gun pointed at Limping Man's head.)*

KENNY.   She doesn't want to go.

LIMPING MAN.   What are you doing?

CLAIRE.   Don't play with guns, honey.

KENNY.   She's not going with you.

LIMPING MAN.   I know you're mad, kiddo. I'm thorry for what I did. I don't know how elthe to thay it to you.

CLAIRE.   Put the gun down, Kenny.

LIMPING MAN.   You know, there wath a time when you couldn't tie your shooth. Do you remember?

KENNY.   She's not going.

LIMPING MAN.   And then I taught you. You remember that thummer at the lake? And now you know how to tie your shooth, right?

KENNY.   Just say you're leaving without her.

LIMPING MAN.   People can learn thingth, Kenny. People can change.

CLAIRE.   Please sweetie, give it to me. *(Pause. Kenny reluctantly hands the gun to her. She throws it out the window.)*

LIMPING MAN.   Uh, I kinda needed that.

CLAIRE.   What'd you do to us?

LIMPING MAN.   I wish you remembered thome of the good thingth.

CLAIRE.   So do I.

LIMPING MAN.   Becauthe, there were … thome good thingth.

CLAIRE.   Yeah, that lake thing you just said sounded nice.

LIMPING MAN.   It wath. And we can go back there. Rent the cottage, get thome inner-toobth, bug thpray — *(Claire seems to have a flash of pain across her head. We hear puppies yapping.)*

KENNY.   Mom?

CLAIRE.   I'm okay. I just … I think I've got one.

KENNY.   One what?

CLAIRE.   *(To Limping Man.)* The first time we met. That's a good one, right?

LIMPING MAN.   Right.

CLAIRE.   I was seventeen.

LIMPING MAN.   Uh-huh.

CLAIRE.   And I came out of school and you were sitting in the front of your pickup with a bunch of puppies on your lap.

KENNY.   Mom, what are you doing?

CLAIRE.   And you were tickling them and making faces. And you saw me and held one up and said, "Ain't this a cute one?" And we smiled at each other. And you reminded me of my father. And I thought, "I'm gonna marry that boy someday. Someone who is so much like my father must be so good inside."

LIMPING MAN.   *(Pause.)* That wathn't me, Claire.

CLAIRE.   What?

LIMPING MAN.   I never had no lap of puppeeth. I'm allergic.

CLAIRE.   Allergic?

LIMPING MAN.   And I never had a pickup either. That wath your dad. That guy reminded you of your dad tho much, becauthe it wath him. I'm allergic to puppeeth.

CLAIRE.   Oh.

LIMPING MAN.   Your couthin Jackie introduthed uth. At the Taco Bell?

CLAIRE.   *(Not remembering.)* Uh-huh.

LIMPING MAN.   Claire …

CLAIRE.   I … I … I'm not going with you.

LIMPING MAN.   But Claire we just had that whole —

CLAIRE.   I can't.

LIMPING MAN.   Is it Kenny? Kenny can come too. I love Kenny. *(To Kenny.)* You wanna come for a ride, kiddo?

CLAIRE.   I feel awful about your ear and the limp and the lisp, and —

LIMPING MAN.   The blindneth.

CLAIRE.   Yeah, your blind eye, I feel bad about that too. But … maybe I didn't have many choices.

LIMPING MAN.   Thweetie …

CLAIRE.   I don't know you. I don't think I ever did. And I don't have any intention of taking up with strangers.

LIMPING MAN.   But thath what you do every morning.

CLAIRE.   I said no.

LIMPING MAN.   *(Pause.)* Okay. No ith no. *(Beat.)* I juth … worked tho hard on thith. *(Moves in closer to her.)* But I underthtand. And I'm thorry. You detherved better. *(He takes her hand affectionately. And, after a beat, bends it back suddenly.)* You ungrateful cunt! *(He's about to hit her, when Kenny leaps on him and punches the wound on his back. The carnival music from earlier scenes blares in.)*

KENNY.   Leave her alone! You piece of shit! *(They struggle for a couple beats, but Philip is no match for Kenny. Kenny beats him into a corner.)*

LIMPING MAN.   I'm thorry, honey! I thlipped!

CLAIRE.   Stop it, Kenny! Please!

LIMPING MAN.   It wath a lapthe. You made me upthet. Aren't I allowed thlipth?! *(Kenny's rage is unrestrained. He kicks Phil, throws things at him. The frozen food. Anything he can grab, he hurls at Phil, who's curled in a ball.)*

KENNY.   After everything, you think you can come back and hit people?!

LIMPING MAN.   I thwear I changed!

58

CLAIRE. Kenny! Don't do that!

LIMPING MAN. My thtitcheth are coming out!

KENNY. Good! *(Hurls things at him.)* Good! Good! Good!

CLAIRE. Kenny! I said stop! You're like him! You're being like him! *(Kenny stops. He's out of breath and spent. The music is gone.)*

LIMPING MAN. *(Defeated, breathless.)* I'm good, Claire. I wath trying. I won't thlip again. Come with me. *(There's suddenly a huge crash and commotion from the basement and stairs.)*

HEIDI. *(Off.)* It's an ambush!

RICHARD. *(Off.)* Get back down here!

GERTIE. *(Off.)* Getta, Record!

HEIDI. *(Off.)* Help me, Phil! *(Then we hear the familiar sound of a shovel being thwacked across someone's head. Heidi staggers in, rubbing her sore head. Richard follows her in, with a poised shovel. She collapses, out cold. Richard whips around and sees the defeated Limping Man.)*

RICHARD. Hey … Hey! You got *him* and I got *her!* You twist his arm, Kenny? Like I taught you?

KENNY. What?

RICHARD. *(Referring to Heidi.)* Look at this one. I smashed her good and hard. *(Beat, then to Claire.)* Are you okay, honey? *(Beat.)* Did I say something?

CLAIRE. Let's just call the police so I can go home. *(Gertie runs into the kitchen with the puppet, pointing at it frantically.)*

GERTIE. Da doopy-guy ish baking pups!

MILLET. *(Off.)* Where's my Binky?!

CLAIRE. Aren't we done yet? I'm so tired. *(Millet enters with hacksaw.)*

MILLET. You gimme my puppet!

GERTIE. *(Throws puppet at him.)* Tay da fuddin puppa.

MILLET. *(To Claire.)* And you gimme that ring!

CLAIRE. *(Gives him ring.)* Here.

RICHARD. Hey, that's my ring.

MILLET. It's *not* your ring! It never was! *(As puppet.)* I missed you, Millet. *(Normal.)* And I missed you, Binky. *(To everyone.)* I'm taking my friend away from you people! *(Puppet.)* Liars and nutsos! *(Normal.)* We're gonna bring this ring back to the owner and clear my name. We'll start over!

LIMPING MAN.   You can't, Millet.

MILLET.   I'll tell them everything! And then they'll believe me! And I'll become a zookeeper! You're bad people! *(Puppet.)* You're all crazy! *(Runs out.)*

RICHARD.   *(Pause.)* There now. That wasn't so bad, was it? You're doing okay, Claire.

CLAIRE.   Richard, don't tell me how I'm doing. Kenny, call the police. Gertie, you'll stay with us tonight.

GERTIE.   Evatin kay nah, Clay. Evatin. Yukabe happy nah. Happy-happy Clay. *(The lights fade on them. The sounds of cars transition us into —)*

SCENE 4

Lights up in the car. Kenny and Gertie are in the backseat. Gertie's asleep. Richard drives. Claire is beside Richard reading from her Filofax book.

RICHARD.   Whataday-whataday-whataday.

CLAIRE.   This book needs to be updated.

RICHARD.   Aye-aye, General.

CLAIRE.   There are a lot of things missing.

RICHARD.   The doctors don't want you to know everything.

CLAIRE.   Why not?

RICHARD.   They said getting that upset every day would take its toll.

CLAIRE.   On who? *(Beat.)* Well, now that I'm fully informed and capable of making decisions, I'm telling you to put it all in. The first sentence: Your deformed husband beat you hard and often.

RICHARD.   This is how you want to start your day?

CLAIRE.   Just put it in.

RICHARD.   You're the boss.

KENNY.   Mom, you remember that blue sweater you made me?

CLAIRE. Sure, sweetie.

KENNY. It has a hole in it. You think you can fix it?

CLAIRE. We'll see.

RICHARD. Look at Gertie. All tuckered out. Been a long day for us, huh Claire?

CLAIRE. How did we get married?

RICHARD. What?

CLAIRE. How did we get married?

RICHARD. Oh. Uhh ... Well, you were in the hospital, and I saw you every day, and eventually I fell in love with you. Your sunny outlook. Your freshness.

KENNY. Your amnesia.

RICHARD. Not just that. Come on, Kenny ...

CLAIRE. And what about *me?*

RICHARD. You?

CLAIRE. Did I agree to marry you?

RICHARD. Not the first eight times I asked. Once we made it as far as the license, and you backed out. But then one day I got lucky. You woke up in that hospital bed, and I was waiting with a cup of coffee and I said, "Good morning, Huckleberry," and you smiled at me. And I told you that I'd been in love with you for many months and we had shared a lot together and would you marry me. And you said okay. And the hospital chaplain came in, and all the paperwork was lined up from the last time, and he married us.

CLAIRE. *(Pause.)* That's weird.

RICHARD. Weird?

CLAIRE. I didn't even know you.

RICHARD. Yes you did, sort of. I asked your mother. Kenny said it was okay.

KENNY. No I didn't. I said I didn't care.

RICHARD. Claire, I love you.

CLAIRE. No, I know. I mean ... you seem nice enough. It's just — I don't know. I'm too tired to think straight.

RICHARD. Okay. *(They drive on in silence. Claire is close to falling asleep.)*

KENNY. Hey, Mom?

CLAIRE. Yeah?

KENNY. Don't go to sleep.

CLAIRE. It's been a long day.

KENNY. I know. I just want a couple more minutes.

CLAIRE. I'm sorry, honey. I'm fading.

RICHARD. Claire?

CLAIRE. Yeah?

RICHARD. What's my name?

CLAIRE. Richard Fiffle.

RICHARD. And who am I?

CLAIRE. *(Pause.)* My husband.

RICHARD. Right. Good. *(Beat.)* You think tomorrow might be different?

CLAIRE. I don't know, Philip.

RICHARD. Richard.

CLAIRE. Right. Richard. *(Beat.)* Fix my book. *(Claire lies back and closes her eyes.)*

RICHARD. Maybe we won't need it. Maybe the alarm'll go off and you'll know me.

KENNY. Maybe you can drive me to school in the morning.

CLAIRE. *(Half-asleep.)* Maybe.

RICHARD. Maybe our lives can go forward now. We can go for a walk in the park if you don't have anything planned.

KENNY. Or the movies.

RICHARD. Maybe tomorrow will be the second day of our marriage. And you'll say something like, "Remember that puppet that crazy guy had?" And I'll say, "Yeah."

KENNY. Maybe you'll remember everything. You think maybe, Mom?

RICHARD. Claire?

KENNY. Mom?

RICHARD. Claire?

KENNY. Mom? *(Silence. Claire's asleep. Richard and Kenny look at each other, then face the front. The lights slowly fade on them staring ahead as they drive into the darkness.)*

END OF PLAY

PROPERTY LIST

Mug of coffee (RICHARD)
Clothes (RICHARD)
Dress (RICHARD)
Puzzle books (RICHARD, CLAIRE)
Purse (KENNY)
Money (KENNY)
Filofax (RICHARD, CLAIRE)
Mirror (RICHARD)
Slippers (CLAIRE)
Dress (LIMPING MAN)
Shoes (LIMPING MAN)
Photo (CLAIRE)
Cup of tea (GERTIE)
Knife (GERTIE)
Dish towel (GERTIE)
Baseball mitt (LIMPING MAN)
Bacon (GERTIE, RICHARD)
Puppet (MILLET, GERTIE)
Hacksaw (LIMPING MAN, MILLET)
Phone (GERTIE)
Candy (LIMPING MAN)
Joint (KENNY)
Gun (HEIDI, KENNY)
Car license and registration (RICHARD)
Jump rope (CLAIRE)
Hula hoop (MILLET)
Kewpie doll (CLAIRE)
Monster mask (CLAIRE)
Squirt gun (CLAIRE)
Cookie tin containing photos, old newspaper article (GERTIE)
Towel (LIMPING MAN)
Photo album (GERTIE)
Sewing kit (GERTIE)

Shovel (GERTIE, RICHARD)
Bandages (CLAIRE)
Needle and thread (LIMPING MAN)
Frozen food (HEIDI)
Ring (CLAIRE)

SOUND EFFECTS

Alarm clock ringing
Cars on a road
Carnival music
Car horn
Screech of a car
Scanning stations on a car radio
'70s easy-listening song
Siren blaring in distance
Dog barking
Gunshot
Sound of shovel hitting someone's head
Overlapping carnival music, dog barking, '70s easy-listening song
and radio scanning
Puppies yapping
Huge crash

TRANSLATION OF GERTIE'S STROKE-TALK

A note on Gertie's speech patterns: Strokes can affect people in countless ways. Language in particular can be dramatically impaired, often resulting in slurred speech or various forms of aphasia. Gertie's disorder is pretty straightforward. Her words are simply jumbled. Syllables are often inverted, and similar-sounding words and sounds are substituted for the intended words. Gertie does not slur her words, talk slowly or have much difficulty speaking. The gibberish comes out effortlessly, without a struggle. Though she occasionally is very deliberate in her attempts to communicate, her speech patterns almost always have the same cadences and rhythms of someone who speaks normally. Gertie usually knows exactly what she's trying to say in a very pointed way, while everyone around her is left to decipher the jumbled sentiments.

ACT ONE, Scene 3

Clay? Whadda dune hay? Youshen be gnome!
Claire? What are you doing here? You should be home!

Income, Clay. Income!
Come in, Claire. Come in!

Fee, whadda helen oodoo?
Philip, what the hell did you do?

Dashen dunder-mince-tate.
That's an understatement.

Fast break, Clay? Eggs? Sear-el? Toe-sat? Fast break?
Breakfast, Claire? Eggs? Cereal? Toast? Breakfast?

Balcony?
Bacon?

I jez hava fidful oh da balcony cuz yo foddeh lie dit so moo. I jez godden haboo oh keeboo da-roun oda tie.
I just have a fridge full of bacon because your father liked it so much. I just got into the habit of keeping some around all the time.

Ina la.
In the cellar.

I doan tink-toe, Clay.
I don't think so, Claire.

Clay, lessco fo wah, kay?
Claire, let's go for a walk, okay?

Isso ny ow sigh, lessco fo wah.
It's so nice outside, let's go for a walk.

Ya, da kenny. Buh Clay, lissa toe-me, peas.
Yeah, the kennel. But Claire, listen to me, please.

No, Clay. Ida know no puppas!
No Claire. I don't know no puppets!

A base-freezer, Clay. Day base-freeze croquet.
A freebaser, Claire. They freebase cocaine.

Clay, noo-noo dish is gooey.
Claire, none of this is good.

Ees med ah noose bah.
These men are bad news.

Clay, dish is nah —
Claire, this is not —

Isis Geht Maso. Fee cape. Eesh ina hiss … Huh? … Fee cape … Cape … Ee brogue adder summer … Fee Cape! … Geht Maso! … Fee cape!!!
This is Gertie Mason. Philip escaped. He's in the house … Huh? … Philip escaped … *Escaped* … He broke out out of the slammer … *Philip escaped!* … Gertie Mason! … *Philip escaped!!!*

Ish da rye? Dah isho fuddy.
Is that right? That is so funny.

Hoe-down do sicken.
Hold on a second.

Iyas mah frient … I cull mah frient … thall.
It was my friend … I called my friend … that's all.

No Fee, yoda ony baddy doo Clay.
No Philip, you've done only bad things to Claire.

ACT ONE, Scene 7

Trush noon by me, Clay.
Trust no one but me, Claire.

Dusha riddle dimsum da my hempoo.
Just a little something that might help you.

I doan tink-toe!
I don't think so!

Dash ny!
That's nice!

Who do teching bat?
Who are you talking about?

Uh-huh. I bee rye bag.
Uh-huh. I'll be right back.

Pen-o, Clay. Toe-phoes.
Open, Claire. Photos.

Ada fay. Ih da fuhnus. Da meers.
At the fair. In the fun house. The mirrors.

Ih da fuhnus. Fuddy meers.
In the fun house. Funny mirrors.

Da Piehmoe Fay.
The Piermont Fair.

An da Za in da fuddy meers.
And that's Zack in the funny mirrors.

Yada tooda pitue oh Za ih da fuddy meers.
Your dad took the picture of Zack in the funny mirrors.

Edadly!
Exactly!

Da ih Za, Clay. He feh oh da tee.
That is Zack, Claire. He fell out of the tree.

You doe mem ohta tins dah happy!
You don't remember all the things that happened!

Yesh! Da fyin pay!
Yes! The frying pan!

Dogdambit!
Goddamnit!

Cursive. Ida nevoo crotch you.
Of course. I'd never cross you.

Noda Za, Clay. Ee feh oh da tee.
That's not Zack, Claire. He fell out of the tree.

Yuca keelush, Fee, buhda woe cha-cha nuddy!
You can kill us, Philip, but it won't change nothin'!

Ree, Clay! Ree!
Read, Claire! Read!

Ih tess wha happy!
It tells what happened!

Egg dis!
Take this!

Isis Geht Maso. Fee Cape! ... *I dabbed him inda bag!*
This is Gertie Mason. *Philip escaped!* ... I stabbed him in the back!

Ona four ohda clickin! Oh, dear heah!
On the floor of the kitchen! Oh, they're here!

No! Iss my-pho! Fug-dew!
No! This is my phone! Fuck you!

Ah! My pho!
Ah! My phone!

Dab da fuddin puppa!
Stab the fuckin' puppet!

Kee da puppa! Doopy fuddin puppa! Die! Die!
Kill the puppet! Stupid fuckin' puppet! Die! Die!

ACT TWO, Scene 1

An noon onion stammy!
And no one understands me!

Ish axel is genderlish!
This asshole is dangerous.

Ee hersh poopoos!
He hurts people!

I doan onion stammish.
I don't understand this.

Ida gnome mower, Clay. Evatin row when Za feh oda tee. Da die. Oomay Fee an bah tin happy. Deh oo fie bah an deh figit. An I hada toke, so king talk bah. Fee heah an evatin bah gin. Evatin bah gin, Clay.
I don't know anymore, Claire. Everything went wrong when Zack fell out of the tree. Dad died. You married Philip and bad things happened. Then you fight back and then forget. And I had a stroke, so I'm talking bad. Philip's back and everything's bad again. Everything's bad again, Claire.

ACT TWO, Scene 2

Dash biggo yoo-zo doopy.
That's because you're so stupid.

Yah. Maybe ova nose bachus.
Yeah. Over in those boxes.

Uh ... oday. Aybee ride bag.
Uh ... okay. I'll be right back.

Nuddin fuddy heah.
Nothing funny here.

Ahm dill loodin!
I'm still looking!

I tink iss up in da clickin.
I think it's up in the kitchen.

I gut da doe-in-tit.
I've got the sewing kit.

Loo ah dese toe-phos, Record.
Look at these photos, Richard.

Loo ah dis one dough. Is da weddin dah.
Look at this one though. It's the wedding day.

Sumna-bitch.
Sonofabitch.

I coo tah den. Bach den evabiddy onion stammy. I wizz-eye hat ... Iiii wiissh ... I had ... sehd sssummttiiinnn weeeehnn ... I c-could.
I could talk then. Back then everybody understood me. I wish I had ... I wish ... I had ... said something when ... I could.

Digga widda shova.
Digging with the shovel.

Aybee rye bag.
I'll be right back.

Toe-phoes! Thall! Toe-phoes!
Photos! That's all! Photos!

Dem pick gog shit! Fuddin shit!
Damn prick goddamn shit! Fucking shit!

72

I'm loodin!
I'm looking!

I ding I fow da bach, Record!
I think I found the box, Richard!

Damma fuddin shova!
Damn this fucking shovel!

I guddit!
I've got it!

ACT TWO, Scene 3

Heddo, dis geddin da doe-in-tit.
Hello, just getting the sewing kit.

I gut da doe-in-tit.
I've got the sewing kit.

Getta, Record!
Get her, Richard!

Da doopy-guy ish baking pups!
The stupid guy is waking up!

Tay da fuddin puppa.
Take the fuckin' puppet.

Evatin kay nah, Clay. Evatin. Yukabe happy nah. Happy-happy Clay.
Everything's okay now, Claire. Everything. You can be happy now.
Happy happy Claire.

DESIGN AND THE WORLD OF THE PLAY

The audience should experience the play through Claire's eyes as much as possible. With that in mind, the world that the designers create should be a world of incomplete pictures and distorted realities. I imagine the set being representational and fluid. Scenes should flow into focus without interruption. Perhaps as the play moves forward and Claire's vision of her world becomes clearer, so too do her surroundings. For example, each time we revisit Gertie's kitchen, maybe there's a new piece of furniture, or there's a wall where there wasn't one before. But ultimately this is a world of mirrors and memories. I imagine perhaps scrims and projections that can easily transform a space.

At the same time, Claire's world is like a funhouse, where anything can happen. A floor can drop. A room can suddenly be filled with noise. Something terrifying can pop out of the darkness. Giddiness can turn into horror at the turn of a corner. By no means do I want the funhouse imagery literally represented on stage, but maybe a few pieces of furniture are a bit oversized or askew (nothing too stylized or cartoonish). Claire lives in an unsettling world where mad fun and genuine danger are wrapped around each other. The design should help bring this world to life, and include the audience on the ride.

NEW PLAYS

★ **THE CREDEAUX CANVAS by Keith Bunin.** A forged painting leads to tragedy among friends. "There is that moment between adolescence and middle age when being disaffected looks attractive. Witness the enduring appeal of Prince Hamlet, Jake Barnes and James Dean, on the stage, page and screen. Or, more immediately, take a look at the lithe young things in THE CREDEAUX CANVAS…" –*NY Times.* "THE CREDEAUX CANVAS is the third recent play about painters…it turned out to be the best of the lot, better even than most plays about non-painters." –*NY Magazine.* [2M, 2W] ISBN: 0-8222-1838-0

★ **THE DIARY OF ANNE FRANK by Frances Goodrich and Albert Hackett, newly adapted by Wendy Kesselman.** A transcendently powerful new adaptation in which Anne Frank emerges from history a living, lyrical, intensely gifted young girl. "Undeniably moving. It shatters the heart. The evening never lets us forget the inhuman darkness waiting to claim its incandescently human heroine." –*NY Times.* "A sensitive, stirring and thoroughly engaging new adaptation." –*NY Newsday.* "A powerful new version that moves the audience to gasps, then tears." –*A.P.* "One of the year's ten best." – *Time Magazine.* [5M, 5W, 3 extras] ISBN: 0-8222-1718-X

★ **THE BOOK OF LIZ by David Sedaris and Amy Sedaris.** Sister Elizabeth Donderstock makes the cheese balls that support her religious community, but feeling unappreciated among the Squeamish, she decides to try her luck in the outside world. "…[a] delightfully off-key, off-color hymn to clichés we all live by, whether we know it or not." –*NY Times.* "Good-natured, goofy and frequently hilarious…" –*NY Newsday.* "…[THE BOOK OF LIZ] may well be the world's first Amish picaresque…hilarious…" –*Village Voice.* [2M, 2W (doubling, flexible casting to 8M, 7W)] ISBN: 0-8222-1827-5

★ **JAR THE FLOOR by Cheryl L. West.** A quartet of black women spanning four generations makes up this hilarious and heartwarming dramatic comedy. "…a moving and hilarious account of a black family sparring in a Chicago suburb…" –*NY Magazine.* "…heart-to-heart confrontations and surprising revelations…first-rate…" –*NY Daily News.* "…unpretentious good feelings…bubble through West's loving and humorous play…" –*Star-Ledger.* "…one of the wisest plays I've seen in ages…[from] a master playwright." –*USA Today.* [5W] ISBN: 0-8222-1809-7

★ **THIEF RIVER by Lee Blessing.** Love between two men over decades is explored in this incisive portrait of coming to terms with who you are. "Mr. Blessing unspools the plot ingeniously, skipping back and forth in time as the details require…an absorbing evening." –*NY Times.* "…wistful and sweet-spirited…" –*Variety.* [6M] ISBN: 0-8222-1839-9

★ **THE BEGINNING OF AUGUST by Tom Donaghy.** When Jackie's wife abruptly and mysteriously leaves him and their infant daughter, a pungently comic reevaluation of suburban life ensues. "Donaghy holds a cracked mirror up to the contemporary American family, anatomizing its frailties and miscommunications in fractured language that can be both funny and poignant." –*The Philadelphia Inquirer.* "…[A] sharp, eccentric new comedy. Pungently funny…fresh and precise…" –*LA Times.* [3M, 2W] ISBN: 0-8222-1786-4

★ **OUTSTANDING MEN'S MONOLOGUES 2001–2002 and OUTSTANDING WOMEN'S MONOLOGUES 2001–2002 edited by Craig Pospisil.** Drawn exclusively from Dramatists Play Service publications, these collections for actors feature over fifty monologues each and include an enormous range of voices, subject matter and characters. MEN'S ISBN: 0-8222-1821-6 WOMEN'S ISBN: 0-8222-1822-4

DRAMATISTS PLAY SERVICE, INC.
440 Park Avenue South, New York, NY 10016 212-683-8960 Fax 212-213-1539
postmaster@dramatists.com www.dramatists.com

NEW PLAYS

★ **A LESSON BEFORE DYING by Romulus Linney, based on the novel by Ernest J. Gaines.** An innocent young man is condemned to death in backwoods Louisiana and must learn to die with dignity. "The story's wrenching power lies not in its outrage but in the almost inexplicable grace the characters must muster as their only resistance to being treated like lesser beings." *—The New Yorker.* "Irresistable momentum and a cathartic explosion...a powerful inevitability." *—NY Times.* [5M, 2W] ISBN: 0-8222-1785-6

★ **BOOM TOWN by Jeff Daniels.** A searing drama mixing small-town love, politics and the consequences of betrayal. "...a brutally honest, contemporary foray into classic themes, exploring what moves people to lie, cheat, love and dream. By BOOM TOWN's climactic end there are no secrets, only bare truth." *—Oakland Press.* "...some of the most electrifying writing Daniels has ever done..." *—Ann Arbor News.* [2M, 1W] ISBN: 0-8222-1760-0

★ **INCORRUPTIBLE by Michael Hollinger.** When a motley order of medieval monks learns their patron saint no longer works miracles, a larcenous, one-eyed minstrel shows them an outrageous new way to pay old debts. "A lightning-fast farce, rich in both verbal and physical humor." *—American Theatre.* "Everything fits snugly in this funny, endearing black comedy...an artful blend of the mock-formal and the anachronistically breezy...A piece of remarkably dexterous craftsmanship." *—Philadelphia Inquirer.* "A farcical romp, scintillating and irreverent." *—Philadelphia Weekly.* [5M, 3W] ISBN: 0-8222-1787-2

★ **CELLINI by John Patrick Shanley.** Chronicles the life of the original "Renaissance Man," Benvenuto Cellini, the sixteenth-century Italian sculptor and man-about-town. Adapted from the autobiography of Benvenuto Cellini, translated by J. Addington Symonds. "[Shanley] has created a convincing Cellini, not neglecting his dark side, and a trim, vigorous, fast-moving show." *—BackStage.* "Very entertaining...With brave purpose, the narrative undermines chronology before untangling it...touching and funny..." *—NY Times.* [7M, 2W (doubling)] ISBN: 0-8222-1808-9

★ **PRAYING FOR RAIN by Robert Vaughan.** Examines a burst of fatal violence and its aftermath in a suburban high school. "Thought provoking and compelling." *—Denver Post.* "Vaughan's powerful drama offers hope and possibilities." *—Theatre.com.* "[The play] doesn't put forth compact, tidy answers to the problem of youth violence. What it does offer is a compelling exploration of the forces that influence an individual's choices, and of the proverbial lifelines—be they familial, communal, religious or political—that tragically slacken when society gives in to apathy, fear and self-doubt..." *—Westword.* "...a symphony of anger..." *—Gazette Telegraph.* [4M, 3W] ISBN: 0-8222-1807-0

★ **GOD'S MAN IN TEXAS by David Rambo.** When a young pastor takes over one of the most prestigious Baptist churches from a rip-roaring old preacher-entrepreneur, all hell breaks loose. "...the pick of the litter of all the works at the Humana Festival..." *—Providence Journal.* "...a wealth of both drama and comedy in the struggle for power..." *—LA Times.* "...the first act is so funny...deepens in the second act into a sobering portrait of fear, hope and self-delusion..." *—Columbus Dispatch.* [3M] ISBN: 0-8222-1801-1

★ **JESUS HOPPED THE 'A' TRAIN by Stephen Adly Guirgis.** A probing, intense portrait of lives behind bars at Rikers Island. "...fire-breathing...whenever it appears that JESUS is settling into familiar territory, it slides right beneath expectations into another, fresher direction. It has the courage of its intellectual restlessness...[JESUS HOPPED THE 'A' TRAIN] has been written in flame." *—NY Times.* [4M, 1W] ISBN: 0-8222-1799-6

DRAMATISTS PLAY SERVICE, INC.
440 Park Avenue South, New York, NY 10016 212-683-8960 Fax 212-213-1539
postmaster@dramatists.com www.dramatists.com

NEW PLAYS

★ **THE CIDER HOUSE RULES, PARTS 1 & 2 by Peter Parnell, adapted from the novel by John Irving.** Spanning eight decades of American life, this adaptation from the Irving novel tells the story of Dr. Wilbur Larch, founder of the St. Cloud's, Maine orphanage and hospital, and of the complex father-son relationship he develops with the young orphan Homer Wells. "...luxurious digressions, confident pacing...an enterprise of scope and vigor..." –*NY Times.* "...The fact that I can't wait to see Part 2 only begins to suggest just how good it is..." –*NY Daily News.* "...engrossing...an odyssey that has only one major shortcoming: It comes to an end." –*Seattle Times.* "...outstanding...captures the humor, the humility...of Irving's 588-page novel..." –*Seattle Post-Intelligencer.* [9M, 10W, doubling, flexible casting] PART 1 ISBN: 0-8222-1725-2 PART 2 ISBN: 0-8222-1726-0

★ **TEN UNKNOWNS by Jon Robin Baitz.** An iconoclastic American painter in his seventies has his life turned upside down by an art dealer and his ex-boyfriend. "...breadth and complexity...a sweet and delicate harmony rises from the four cast members...Mr. Baitz is without peer among his contemporaries in creating dialogue that spontaneously conveys a character's social context and moral limitations..." –*NY Times.* "...darkly funny, brilliantly desperate comedy...TEN UNKNOWNS vibrates with vital voices." –*NY Post.* [3M, 1W] ISBN: 0-8222-1826-7

★ **BOOK OF DAYS by Lanford Wilson.** A small-town actress playing St. Joan struggles to expose a murder. "...[Wilson's] best work since *Fifth of July*...An intriguing, prismatic and thoroughly engrossing depiction of contemporary small-town life with a murder mystery at its core...a splendid evening of theater..." –*Variety.* "...fascinating...a densely populated, unpredictable little world." –*St. Louis Post-Dispatch.* [6M, 5W] ISBN: 0-8222-1767-8

★ **THE SYRINGA TREE by Pamela Gien.** Winner of the 2001 Obie Award. A breathtakingly beautiful tale of growing up white in apartheid South Africa. "Instantly engaging, exotic, complex, deeply shocking...a thoroughly persuasive transport to a time and a place...stun[s] with the power of a gut punch..." –*NY Times.* "Astonishing...affecting ...[with] a dramatic and heartbreaking conclusion...A deceptive sweet simplicity haunts THE SYRINGA TREE..." –*A.P.* [1W (or flexible cast)] ISBN: 0-8222-1792-9

★ **COYOTE ON A FENCE by Bruce Graham.** An emotionally riveting look at capital punishment. "The language is as precise as it is profane, provoking both troubling thought and the occasional cheerful laugh...will change you a little before it lets go of you." –*Cincinnati CityBeat.* "...excellent theater in every way..." –*Philadelphia City Paper.* [3M, 1W] ISBN: 0-8222-1738-4

★ **THE PLAY ABOUT THE BABY by Edward Albee.** Concerns a young couple who have just had a baby and the strange turn of events that transpire when they are visited by an older man and woman. "An invaluable self-portrait of sorts from one of the few genuinely great living American dramatists...rockets into that special corner of theater heaven where words shoot off like fireworks into dazzling patterns and hues." –*NY Times.* "An exhilarating, wicked...emotional terrorism." –*NY Newsday.* [2M, 2W] ISBN: 0-8222-1814-3

★ **FORCE CONTINUUM by Kia Corthron.** Tensions among black and white police officers and the neighborhoods they serve form the backdrop of this discomfiting look at life in the inner city. "The creator of this intense...new play is a singular voice among American playwrights...exceptionally eloquent..." –*NY Times.* "...a rich subject and a wise attitude." –*NY Post.* [6M, 2W, 1 boy] ISBN: 0-8222-1817-8

DRAMATISTS PLAY SERVICE, INC.
440 Park Avenue South, New York, NY 10016 212-683-8960 Fax 212-213-1539
postmaster@dramatists.com www.dramatists.com